WITHDRAWN

David Ricardo

Columbia Essays on the Great Economists
Donald J. Dewey, General Editor

◄►◄►◄►

David

RICARDO

◄►◄►◄►

Michael J. Gootzeit

COLUMBIA UNIVERSITY ♔ NEW YORK AND LONDON
PRESS   1975

Library of Congress Cataloging in Publication Data

Gootzeit, Michael J., 1939–
   David Ricardo.
   (Columbia essays on the great economists)
   Bibliography: p.
1. Ricardo, David, 1772–1823.
        HB103.R5G66   330.15'3'0924   75–5687
            ISBN 0–231–03524–1
            ISBN 0–231–03916–6 pbk.

Contents

Preface

David Ricardo's economic writings were accomplished in the short span of fourteen years—from 1809 to 1823. But it would be difficult to select another writer in any field who exerted such a strong influence on its ultimate development. However, it is sometimes difficult for modern students of economics, from a 150-year perspective, to pinpoint Ricardo's main contributions to the science. This is because his ideas have become so thoroughly integrated with the logical building blocks formulated by other writers that the true originality of his contributions is difficult to define. Furthermore, many errors of exposition crept into Ricardo's works. These can generally be conceived as either errors of logic, errors of omission, or errors of consistency. Many later economists (including myself) have occupied themselves with research efforts in order to point out how the essential Ricardian system was constructed and, in retrospect, what was wrong with it. This examination of the Ricardian system has therefore identified and corrected some of the "important" errors in the initial exposition.

Utilizing this analytical approach, we can also discover the "basic" elements of the Ricardian system. Ricardo's views on the major topics to which he devoted his attention can be examined and, simultaneously, the imperfect nature of his arguments can be pointed out. Many of these problems will be seen to arise because of errors of consistency in Ricardo's method of approach. Over the years, as his theories developed and his powers of analysis improved, Ricardo would change his opinion regarding certain critical points of his theoretical system. This change of opinion might go through several stages and even vacillate from one position to its opposite and back again. We shall see an example of this phenomenon below when we discuss Ricardo's theory of wages.

Another source of difficulty in the exposition of Ricardo's system which caused an inconsistent approach is the arbitrary nature of the political process, to whose winds of change Ricardo quickly adjusted his analytical powers. Whichever economic problem was of national concern was of paramount importance to Ricardo, who developed prescriptions for the treatment of the difficulty. Since he generally took a position which was opposed by politically powerful special interest groups, his arguments had to be neatly concise and simply stated. They also had to be published in organs which would reach the upper-middle-class readers who had the most influence on government decision making. Therefore, the great majority of Ricardo's public writings appeared either in soft-cover pamphlet form or in letters to a newspaper. They were written in a clear expository style with a great emphasis given to conclusions and a smaller emphasis given to the logical process by which the conclusions were derived. Contradictions were avoided by carefully overlooking to consider "exceptions" to the general rule that was being established. This practical situation also caused Ricardo to lay down his economic system in bits and pieces (a newspaper article here, a pamphlet there, a book of principles to emphasize several previous contributions) while never thoroughly integrating the elements for later generations. This is the greatest weakness of the Ricardian system. It is therefore the difficulty which we shall discuss first. It will be shown that a more careful formulation of its basic elements would have saved the Ricardian system from one of its most fundamental weaknesses—the lack of integration between the monetary and real sectors of the economy.

David Ricardo

‹ 1 ›

The Money Market Versus the Output Market

Almost all current (in the last fifteen years) research efforts on Ricardo concentrate on the system he developed to explain the nature of value and production in the economy and how

The produce of the earth—all that is derived from its surface by the united application of labour, machinery, and capital, is divided among three classes of the community; namely, the proprietor of the land, the owner of the stock of capital necessary for its cultivation, and the labourers by whose industry it is cultivated. (*Works*, 1:5.)

This paragraph comes from the preface to Ricardo's *Principles* and it is a good summary of the most important elements discussed in this work. The *Principles* is the most formal of all Ricardo's economic writings. It was carefully thought out and composed and was to contain in a more enlarged and comprehensive fashion the basic elements of an earlier pamphlet: "Essay on Profits." (See *Works*, 1:xiii.) Since a large segment of the audience to which the *Principles* was directed were well-educated, it was written according to a high scholarly standard, replete with numerical examples and carefully reasoned logical statements. It has been the favorite topic of later analyses because it was thought to contain the most complete and formal statement of what Ricardo regarded as important.

Even though the production and distribution system explained in the *Principles* has provided most of the raw material for current research into the relationship between Ricardian and modern economics, there is another important area of concern to which Ricardo made many valuable contributions. This was the great debate taking place in England during the early years of the nineteenth century concerning how the government could best finance the Napoleonic wars on the continent while maintaining stability in the domestic economy. The rigid gold standard which was the basis of the international payments mechanism prevailing among the major European countries at the time meant that large foreign expenditures would have to be settled by gold flows from England to the continent, while domestic convertibility of paper money meant that a sufficient supply of gold should be maintained at home. Both these urgent demands for gold were too great for the small supply of gold possessed by the Bank of England, and the government passed a law in 1797 prohibiting the Bank from redeeming its notes in gold. (Viner, *Studies*, p. 122.) This legislation, which remained in effect until 1819, put England on an inconvertible paper standard. (Ibid., pp. 136 and 145.) Prices rose during the period from 1797 to 1814 and the paper pound depreciated in foreign exchange while a negative balance of payments prevailed.*

---

*The actual index of general commodity prices rose 40% during this period. The rise was discontinuous as was the fall from 1814 to 1818. Between 1818 and 1830, however, prices fell continuously. See: N. Silberling, "British Prices and Business Cycles, 1779–1850," *Review of Economic Statistics*, Oct. 1923, pp. 223–62.

Ricardo was one of the leading economists of the period who tried to explain the evil effects of the Bank restriction which took England off the gold standard. He was called a "bullionist" because he tried to show that the return to gold payments by the Bank would lead to a smoothly expanding national economy. Continued inconvertibility could only lead to the decline of England's status as an international financial power and (even more important) to the weakening of her great potential for economic expansion.

The exact role of the "bullionist" controversy in Ricardo's economic analysis will be explained below, but for now let it suffice to say that this pressing political problem was the reason for Ricardo's first appearance in print. The majority of Ricardo's writings, in fact, were concerned with problems concerning England's monetary system. His initial statements were published in 1809 as three letters to a newspaper—the *Morning Chronicle*. His subsequent monetary analysis was also confined to what could be called the "periodical" literature. Most of it was contained in pamphlets published for an audience of businessmen and legislators. It was highly polemical in style, for its main purpose was to convince those in an influential position that more positive control should be exerted on the paper note issuing authority of the Bank of England. This prescription was eventually accepted by Parliament, but only after ten years had elapsed and the problem Ricardo was referring to had largely declined in practical importance. But since, while expounding this policy, Ricardo was also discussing important principles of economics, some of which eventually found their way into more modern controversies, it is worthwhile for us to examine more closely the major problem in the construction of his monetary system.

This problem is related to the arbitrary separation by Ricardo of the money market from the output market. This lack of integration of the two major sectors of the economy is one of the greatest criticisms of classical economics in general and it is glaringly apparent in some of Ricardo's formulations. Ricardo initially realized that in order to have a consistent approach in his analysis of goods he should examine simultaneously the relationship between money and other commodities produced:

> It is particularly worthy of observation that so deep-rooted is the prejudice which considers coin and bullion as things essentially differing in all their operations from other commodities, that writers greatly enlightened upon the general truth of political economy seldom fail, after having requested their readers to consider money and bullion merely as commodities subject to "the same general principle of supply and demand which are unquestionably the foundation on which the superstructure of political economy is built," to forget this recommendation themselves, and to argue upon the subject of money, and the laws which regulate its export and import, as quite distinct and different from those which regulate the export and import of other commodities. ("High Price of Bullion," Appendix, 1811. *Works*, 3:103–4.)

But by the time he had written his Principles in 1817, the analysis of the real sector became his primary object of concern while the description of the monetary sector was relegated to chapter 27 in the last quarter of the book. Moreover, this chapter was artificially separated from the remainder of the book, which contained a strong emphasis on the analysis of production and distribution:

> Chapter 27, "On Currency and Banks," seems to stand apart from the rest of the book, and, unfortunately, gives an entirely inadequate impression of Ricardo's theory of money. (Blaug, *Economic Theory in Retrospect*, p. 134.)

Ricardo's rigid separation of the money and output markets can be emphasized by briefly observing the theory of value he expounded in his *Principles*. There are really two theories of value in the *Principles*: A. The rather simple and unadorned labor cost theory. B. The more complicated capital/labor theory which was initially developed as an "exception" to A in the third edition of the *Principles*, but which, because of recent research efforts, has become endowed with a life of its own. The discussion here will center on A and show how this straightforward conception of value led to the separation of the output and money markets in Ricardian economics.

Chapters 2, 5, and 6 (the chapters on rent, wages, and profits, respectively) of Ricardo's *Principles* utilized a rather complicated numerical illustration (set in agriculture) to summarize the major points which were made regarding the relationship of the three components of total product. It was Ricardo's idea to show how, as income expanded, the distributive share of each of the three social classes changed relative to one another. The absolute size of each income share was calculated, both in money and in wheat terms, before the three shares were compared, however. Ricardo wanted to use money as well as wheat quantities because he wanted to be as realistic as possible. He knew that inflation could be a problem from previous studies of monetary phenomena and he wanted to be sure to study its effects. Therefore, he assumed that the price of wheat was set initially at £4 per quarter, when cultivation of domestic farm land was extended only as far as the most fertile grade. This grade of land produced 180 quarters of wheat when one dose of capital/labor was applied. When an increase in demand for wheat forced cultivation onto less fertile domestic land (on which only 170 quarters of wheat could be produced by an identical dose of capital/labor) the simple labor theory of value illustrated how the price of wheat would rise. Since the exchange value of a uniform commodity varied in proportion to the standard labor embodied in its production, and since diminishing marginal product occurred in the production of wheat, the value of wheat (per standard unit) must have been rising. Ricardo illustrated how the value of wheat would rise as follows: Originally (when only land of the first quality was being cultivated), 1/180 units of labor was embodied in each quarter of wheat. When land of the second quality was finally used, 1/170 units of labor was the amount needed to produce each quarter of wheat. Therefore, the amount of labor embodied within one unit of wheat increased by 18/17, so the value of this commodity must have increased by this ratio. Ricardo showed the price of wheat rising to, £4.4.8 = 18/17 (£4). (*Works*, 1:83n.)

The numerical example continued along these lines and illustrated how the price of wheat rising when agricultural production was expanding in the economy caused certain undesirable effects on the three income classes mentioned above. These results will be discussed later; for the present we would like to emphasize that Ricardo was discussing an inflationary situation without reference to the money supply or any other monetary phenomenon. He could only do this by assuming that the value of money remained constant while the value of farm goods was increasing no matter what happened to the supply of money. Thus, money would be a perfect measuring rod for true (labor) value. Ricardo assumed away the stock of money as a determinant of commodity prices in his *Principles*, Chapter 1 (On Value), Section 6 (On an invariable measure of value), when he supposed that monetary gold was produced under conditions of constant returns:

> . . . by far the most important effects (on the value of commodities) are produced by the varying quantities of labour required for production; and therefore, if we suppose this important cause of variation removed from the production of gold, we shall probably possess as near an approximation to a standard measure of value as can be theoretically conceived. (*Works*, 1:45.)

When gold was produced under conditions of constant returns, any variation in the level of commodity prices in the economy was caused by a change in the labor value of goods in production, not by a change in the labor value of the monetary medium. The stock of money may expand or contract, but if the amount of labor embodied within each output unit remained the same, the quantity of the money in existence would have no effect on the commodity price level. Prices in the output market were thus determined exclusively by the relative labor content of commodities and not by the supply of money in existence.

But what about determining the value of money itself? Merely asserting that the monetary medium may be assumed to be produced under conditions of constant returns gives no clue as to how its value should be determined. This was not a question which received a satisfactory answer in the *Principles*. But it was a problem to which Ricardo addressed himself to a large degree in many of his other writings. For example, note the following statement from "Reply to Mr. Bosanquet's Practical Observations on the Report of the Bullion Committee," 1811:

> If in addition be made to a currency consisting partly of gold and partly of paper, by an increase of paper currency the value of the whole currency would be diminished, or, in other words, the prices of commodities would rise, estimated either in gold coin or in paper currency. The same commodity would purchase, after the increase of paper, a greater number of ounces of gold coin, because it would exchange for a greater quantity of money. (*Works*, 3:210–11.)

This statement shows that Ricardo utilized the crude quantity theory of money to uniquely determine the value of money. The absolute price level was thus determined exclusively in the money market by specifying that it varied in direct proportion to the supply of money in existence. The money supply thus took on an importance in the determination of the absolute price level which it never had in the determination of relative commodity prices.

This argument shows that the money and output markets were kept rigidly separated, because in the latter Ricardo attached the measure of value function to the monetary medium, while in the former the size of the standard monetary measure was being determined. Most later economists have regarded this separation as artificial and misleading. A reaction against this process was one of the main reasons for the refinement of monetary theory that led to the Keynesian revolution. The "dichotomization of the pricing process," as it has been called, can be described in the following terms:

> According to Lange and Patinkin, the classics nevertheless sought to dichotomize the pricing process by determining relative prices in the "real sector" of the economy and absolute prices by introducing an additional relationship. . . the quantity theory of money. This relates the quantity of money which people wish to hold to the price level by postulating that the quantity of cash the public demands will rise with absolute prices. (Becker and Baumol, p. 359.)

◄ 2 ►

Say's Law and the Bullionist Controversy

      The construction of Ricardo's *Principles* tended to justify the artificial dichotomization of the monetary and real sectors of the economy described above and unfortunately this is the picture of his system afforded by most textbooks. Ricardo maintained this distinction because he regarded the *Principles* as a convenient organ in which to emphasize the theory he had developed two years before in his "Essay on Profits" (*Works*, 4:1–41.) to deal with his production system. As such, he apparently did not think it necessary to include a carefully coordinated analysis of his monetary system, which was more descriptive than theoretical. Moreover, even though Ricardo preferred to publish this policy-oriented material in pamphlets rather than in book form, in order to gain a larger audience, his many contributions to the pamphlet literature clearly indicate that he devoted a large proportion of his total attention to monetary problems. Therefore, we should question the modern practices of emphasizing his contributions to production theory. Furthermore, contained within Ricardo's monetary analysis, we can find the kernels of several important principles about the real sector of the economy—some of which are still important in modern economics. The impression that one gets from reading his *Principles*, that Ricardo tended to maintain an arbitrary separation between the money and the output market, is therefore removed by examining some of his monetary works.

Ricardo's monetary system contained an attack on the Bank Restriction Act of 1797. He believed that this legislation, which took England off the gold standard, was the root cause of certain basic structural difficulties in the real sector of the economy. Ricardo attacked the Bank of England for unfairly taking advantage of this legislation by issuing inconvertible paper currency to excess, so that profitable loans could be made to the government and private sectors of the economy. Ricardo objected because these loans were immensely profitable to the Bank even though the Bank was placed in the position of a "lender of last resort" at the pleasure of the government. Furthermore, even though an excess demand for credit seemed to exist in the money market, the accommodating influence of the Bank increased the supply of credit (and thus the money supply) much too rapidly to suit conditions in the production sector of the economy. Like other "bullionists," Ricardo was always striving to show the evil effects caused by a paper currency that was expanding too quickly. His specific arguments emphasized the close connection between the money supply and the price level. He then proceeded to show how a rapidly rising price level could cause internal adjustment problems in the economy. Professor Viner clearly stated Ricardo's position:

The bullionists argued, or more often simply asserted, that a circulation exceeding in amount what, under otherwise like conditions, could have been maintained under a metallic standard, was in excess.

The only test from English prices alone of the existence of depreciation which he could consistently have accepted, therefore, would have been a comparison of the prices prevailing under inconvertibility with the prices prevailing under convertibility, other conditions remaining the same, and in his treatment of arguments from price data Ricardo always adhered to this position. (Viner, *Studies*, pp. 125 and 127.)

This section will present a summary of the arguments Ricardo advanced during the bullionist controversy to show the effects of a maladjusted money supply on the real sector of the economy. Thus, we will demonstrate that Ricardo had a more sophisticated view regarding integration of the macroeconomic sectors than he would be given credit for if one merely examined his *Principles* models. This generalized view of the economy will be shown to depend to a large degree on the importance given Say's Law in the exposition of his system. It will be demonstrated that Ricardo expounded two versions of this Law and that his conception of general equilibrium can be related to the version discussed most carefully in his writings criticizing the English monetary system.

The basic principle behind Say's Law may be stated quite succinctly:

In an economy with a developed division of labor the means normally available to anyone for acquiring goods and services is the power to produce equivalent goods and services. Production increases not only the supply of goods but, by virtue of the requisite cost payments to the factors of production, also creates the demand to purchase these goods. "Products are paid for by products" in domestic as much as in foreign trade; this is the gist of Say's Law of Markets. (Blaug, *Economic Theory*, p. 145.)

The output market clearing mechanism implicit in Say's Law had its basis in a primitive agricultural society in which barter was the principal means by which goods were exchanged for one another. Output market equilibrium could thus be regarded as the intuitive norm by early writers who used such an economy as a good example of reality. By the time Ricardo wrote, however, the effect of money in the distribution of newly produced goods had become important. Nevertheless, part of his writings were devoted to minimizing the impact of money on the economy by showing how it could be assigned a passive role in the commodity circulation process. Thus, the influence of the monetary sector was diminished and a smoothly functioning (equilibrium) economy could be explained by exclusive reference to the real sector.

Therefore, Ricardo's writings contained a version of Say's Law in which the neutrality of money was emphasized. The exclusive function of money was as a unit of account to facilitate commerce in an industrial economy. The money supply, in fact, was tailored to the quantity to goods produced in the economy:

> Money cannot call forth goods, but goods can call forth money. . . . Here again it is supposed that the augmentation of money procedes the augmentation of goods. I am of opinion however that it would seldom cause any augmentation of goods. . . . that the augmentation of goods is the only legitimate cause for an increase of money. . . . (*Works*, 3:301–2.)

Economic growth could proceed without any cyclic disturbances related to overproduction if the money supply was regarded as a dependent variable. New commodities required that money be injected into the market to facilitate their sale. If the money supply was increased in just the correct proportion, the newly produced goods would be consumed and no complications would occur.

The interpretation of Say's Law just described, which treated the money supply as a dependent variable and asserted that the "real" economy could grow smoothly by establishing the needs of trade for the circulating medium, could regard equilibrium in the money market as a certainty as long as equilibrium was maintained in the output market of the economy. All the money in existence was simply tailored to purchase all the commodities produced. New goods would be circulated with just the right amount of new money. Thus, the money market was subordinated to the output market and money did not take an active role in helping to establish goals for future production levels. This was a comparative statics description of expansion in which positions of disequilibrium were neglected in favor of illustrating sustained economic growth. The price level was not necessarily determined and, furthermore, it was not important as long as this gradually expanding economy that was being described was permanently in equilibrium.

Becker and Baumol have categorized this version of Say's Law, in which the money market was always in benign equilibrium with respect to the remainder of the economy, as Say's Identity. Since the price level played no role in the establishment of money market equilibrium: "Money is a 'veil' since a good can have importance in the determination of equilibrium in the various markets of an economy only if the market for this good can conceivably be out of equilibrium." (Becker and Baumol, p. 358.)

The "bullionist" philosophy included in Ricardo's writings on money seemed to be neglected in this simplified version of Say's Law which showed how the money supply could be exactly accommodated to the needs of commerce. But Ricardo's prescriptions for the regulation of the monetary sector also contained a more sophisticated version which focused quite clearly on the policy measures he thought should be instituted. This analysis emphasized the coordination problems inherent in precisely matching the money supply to the needs of trade. He believed that if too little money was created, problems of lagging sales would become apparent; while if too much money was added, inflation might cause certain serious structural maladjustments. These were difficulties related to disequilibrium. Moreover, they showed a well-defined dynamic relationship between the money and output markets of the economy.

Ricardo's criticism of the Bank of England was not based on the policy of increasing the money supply because, as we have just shown, he believed that it should increase to some extent; he objected instead to the rather rapid rate of increase, maintained under inconvertibility, which led to unwaranted price rises. Ricardo believed inflation could cause misallocation of investment funds and therefore could reduce the pace at which a nation could expand its economic facilities. Therefore, it could cause transformation from an agricultural to an industrial state to be seriously delayed. We shall now analyze the attack Ricardo launched against the monetary authorities by demonstrating the interdependence he constructed between the sectors of the economy when discussing this second version of Say's Law.

Ricardo's monetary writings contained a prominent argument neglected in his other works concerning how equilibrium in the money market could cause the real sector of the economy to be out of equilibrium. Thus, we can no longer take it for granted that the economy would expand smoothly as we did when Ricardo's version of Say's Identity was being described. The economic world was instead regarded more realistically as one in which forward and backward movements occurred together so that expansion of any sector was compensated for by a partial contraction. The net gain remained but was made difficult to attain because price rises interfered with the market clearing mechanism. Certain adjustments to the inflationary situation would have to be made in order for the market to become more efficiently functioning and then rapid progress could continue. But valuable time would be lost before the full potential of the economy for growth could be finally realized, and large segments of the population would be treated unjustly by the delay. This was an analysis which contained basic elements regarding the cyclic nature of the economy to which the name of Malthus rather than Ricardo is generally attached. Nevertheless, if one carefully examines Ricardo's writings of the Bank Restriction period, one can find substantial evidence that he was well aware of acute disequilibrium problems that might arise as the economy grew. Even though he tended to gloss over these difficulties, preferring instead to emphasize equilibrium as a final resting place in some of his other major works, when he was placed in the position of formulating arguments against the policies of what he regarded as the frivolous monetary authorities of the time, his most powerful attacks came in the form of logical salvos which illustrated the *immediate* woes these policies would reap on the economy. Even if the antidote was easy to apply so that the economy could become smoothly functioning again, irreparable damage to the potential for future growth might have taken place.

Ricardo illustrated an inverse relationship between rapidly rising prices and the potential of the economy for growth. The redistribution effect of inflation on wealth and on the flow of earned income would cause this problem. He perceived that the net gain to profits of businessmen who were generally debtors ("farmers, manufacturers, and merchants") from rising prices would be greatly outweighed by the loss to "those who live upon fixed incomes." Moreover, he doubted the wisdom of Malthus' analysis (*Edinburgh Review*, Feb. 1811.) which concluded that (real) net national wealth could be increased only by an inflationary policy. He believed that investment funds would be voluntarily funneled to businessmen by private savers of a moderate (albeit fixed) income who were not directly involved in business projects thereby keeping the money supply and the price level nearly constant. This would be an alternative preferable to the inflationary (money supply increasing) business loans made by the Bank of England. The mechanism by which the private (non-banking) sector could provide all the requisite financing for new business projects was never made clear but it seemed to depend at least partly on the belief that a large enough supply of idle funds existed in the money market which would be used for speculative purposes given a sufficiently high interest rate. (Shades of Keynes!) (See *Works*, 3:122.)

Ricardo argued against utilizing the facilities of the Bank of England to prop the market for commercial loans because of the undesirable welfare effects of inflation on the various segments of the population described above. Furthermore, a little-noticed portion of the argument explained those ill effects using reasoning of a surprisingly modern character. It took into account the fact that business profits would only be increased temporarily by inflation. Expectations of future profits increases would lead businessmen to prematurely expand their production facilities by making new investments too rapidly. Ricardo perceived that the supply of investment funds for these projects would be provided by the process of involuntary or "forced," rather than voluntary, saving.* This could cause a maladjustment in the output market and a temporary surplus of commodities might be produced.

*Ricardo never actually used the term, "forced saving," however.

Let us briefly investigate the reasoning behind this interesting result: The output market of the Ricardian economy was always operating at or close to full employment. Therefore, some "frictional" problems existed when expansion was being described. The movement from one position of equilibrium to a new one at a higher level of production meant that employment would also be greater. But Ricardo realized that there would be a transitional lag between the decision to expand production at one position of full employment and the time when the labor force could grow to meet the new demand so that full employment could be reestablished. During this period an excess demand for labor would prevail, as would an excess demand for the wherewithal to support labor (circulating capital). What did the ability of the Bank of England to enlarge the paper money supply by discounting commercial notes have to do with Ricardo's analysis of the expanding economy?

The Bank of England set off the chain of events leading to the uneven growth of production described above by giving the competitive advantage of new funds to selected firms who were anxious to expand their facilities. These firms would compete for the available labor supply and the complementary circulating capital. The money wage rate as well as the prices of most food staples would rise in the economy. The general price rise would cause the real income and consumption of those who live on fixed earnings to fall. Resources were therefore bidded away from a large class of consumers by prospective producers who were the recipients of the newly created money of the Bank. Part of the previously consumed earnings of this income class were therefore transformed into ("forced") savings. This was the gist of Ricardo's argument concerning how inflation could cause forced savings to take place. Let us now examine the reasoning which showed how this result of monetary mismanagement by the Bank of England would cause the output market to become disproportionately expanded.

Ricardo argued that a lack of coordination between producers and consumers during the transitional period from one position of full employment to the next caused certain commodities to be

produced over-abundantly while other goods became relatively
scarce. This was described as an effect of inertia in the money-
economy when the desire and the expectation of increased profits
caused producers of manufactured goods (conveniences) to enlarge
their production facilities. If expansion took place with full employment and forced savings occurred as described above, part of
the market for most conveniences (including those produced in the
growing sectors of the economy) would be reduced until tastes
had time to change.* Thus, while business expectations might
favor a policy of attempting to increase sales, part of the market
for the manufacturing firms' product must be extinguished simultaneously with increased production. Optimistic business expectations became self-defeating because of rigidities inherent in the
description of full employment. At the same time that conveniences were over-produced, necessities were under-supplied because of the increased competition for circulating capital. (Speech
in the House of Commons, April 1821, *Works*, 5:107–8.)† Equilibrium in the money market was maintained during this adjustment
process by absorption of newly created money into the economy
as prices rose.

Ricardo attempted to illustrate in the analysis just described
how the commodity market could be temporarily out of equilibrium while inflation was occurring. Equilibrium in the output
market could be regained only after a period of time had elapsed
and the production of necessities (food) and conveniences (manufactured goods) had the opportunity to expand in a complemen-

---

*The market for conveniences would be partially extinguished, at least in the
short run, because the standard of living of those who were living on fixed
incomes had been reduced. Furthermore, even if the real wage rate was allowed to
increase, the demand of the working class for goods never before consumed would
be slow to develop.

†The preceding discussion of short run disequilibrium in the Ricardian system
is based on this selection, in which most of the argument presented above is only
briefly stated. Furthermore, it has only recently been published in an easily
available source by Mr. Sraffa. Even though all the basic elements of the theoretical argument against smooth long run expansion of the economy are contained in
this reference, its brevity and its relatively obscure nature should be noted so that
one does not get the impression that Ricardo gave high priority to cyclical
analysis.

tary fashion. Possible population growth implied that the supply of workers to industry would be increasing as manufacturing continued to enlarge. The circulating capital required to support a larger labor force would also be provided, and thus the farm sector would be expanding. This adjustment process would continue until prices and money wages eventually stopped increasing. The class of consumers for industrial goods would be augmented during this interval mainly by a slowly rising standard of living for workers. This was the comparative statics analysis Ricardo provided to logically unify his concepts of stable equilibrium on the one hand and disturbances generated by growth of the economy on the other.

Note that the beginning and end points of the analysis of an increase in money supply illustrate relative neutrality with respect to the total welfare of society. The final growth of the economy simply meant that a larger population shared a larger income in some partially specified fashion. The share of laborers and capitalists may have increased relative to those who lived on fixed incomes, but it is not clear from this result how total welfare would have changed. During the process of adjustment to the increase in paper money, however, fixed income earners and capitalists simultaneously were injured by the inflationary situation. Ricardo was arguing vehemently against this effect of credit expansion. He regarded any positive effect for workers as relatively unimportant compared to the negative influence of rising prices on businessmen and pensioners.

The Ricardian analysis just discussed no longer takes it for granted that supply must necessarily and immediately create its own demand. Thus, as soon as Ricardo stressed that deviations from equilibrium throughout an expanding economy can and do occur, the simple version of Say's Law to which his name is normally ascribed no longer is relevant. These imperfections in the system of production and distribution were shown to be related to a lack of coordination between the policies advocated by the monetary authorities and the actual condition of effective demand and size of plant in the output market. The independence of the real and money sectors of the economy previously discussed no longer held when he emphasized this more complicated description of full employment growth. We can assert that Ricardo's monetary writings exhibited a "sophisticated" version of Say's Law because his analysis of the market clearing relationship in a growing inflationary economy concentrated on short run maladjustments generated from the money to the output market. Overall equilibrium could only occur after these difficulties were corrected as the economy grew over a period of time.

◄3►

Ricardo's Failure as a Practical Monetary Economist

The criticism Ricardo leveled at the Bank of England for maintaining an inflationary monetary policy has been discussed in the last few pages. It was shown that Ricardo believed inflation to cause certain undesirable effects on the classes of the economy responsible for providing the flow of funds required for future growth. When the steady supply of investment funds was interrupted, the expansion of the economy would be delayed and the potential to attain high levels of income might be reduced. Even though most of Ricardo's writings on the subject of money were devoted to demonstrating how inflation could be dangerous, he also gave some effort to explaining how it could be brought under control. He discussed a plan to ameliorate the inflation which had been so prominent in early nineteenth-century England and which both bullionist and anti-bullionist writers agreed was damaging the home economy. The basis of Ricardo's plan was the return to domestic convertibility of paper currency into gold, the idea which lay at the heart of the bullionist economic philosophy. But Ricardo's idea of how convertibility should be reinstituted was eminently practical compared to some of the other schemes put forward. It was so well received by Parliament, in fact, that it was adopted by an act of 1819. Let us look more closely at Ricardo's so-called "Ingot Plan" to see why it was so appealing to the politicans of his day.

The basic element of the Ingot Plan was that the currency to be used for most domestic purchases would remain paper. Gold coins would not substitute for small bank-notes; instead the main supply of gold could be freed for use in settling international debts. Ricardo regarded paper rather than coin as the appropriate medium for domestic circulation because if a persistently negative balance of payments caused the pound to fall below parity on the foreign exchange market, coin could be illegally melted and shipped abroad causing a shortage for official transactions. Coins could also be clipped and deteriorate in value to a large extent over a period of time. ("Appendix to the High Price of Bullion," *Works*, 3:125–27.) Ricardo realized that for England to remain on the gold standard with a paper circulation to be used to settle daily transactions the Bank should be obliged to sell only relatively large units of the precious metal to private parties. Hence, the name "Ingot" plan. Thus, gold could be obtained by the public in exchange for bank notes, but it would be in the form of bullion rather than coin and would only be suitable for hoarding.

The Ingot Plan as accepted by Parliament in 1819 was only a temporary measure until a full gold standard could be instituted. The ingots were made of 60 ounces of gold of a standard fineness, and when they were first sold in February 1820, the price of gold was fixed at 81s. per ounce. They were called "Ricardoes" after their inventor. (P. Sraffa, *Works*, 5:368–69.) Unfortunately, these gold bars never proved very popular because deflation was occurring when they were manufactured and the market price of gold fell below the mint price. Only 13 of 2,028 bars minted were ever sold before full convertibility was resumed in 1823.

Ricardo saw in his plan for the re-installation of domestic

convertibility a method to counteract some of the effects of the rapid inflation which had enveloped England. He believed his plan would lead to a firmer control by the government of the circulating domestic money supply. Since the paper money supply had been overexpanded, he thought that active sales of gold from the coffers of the Bank of England should occur. This would reduce the amount of paper money in circulation and the price level would fall almost immediately. Large relative price variations could be avoided by using such leverage so that only a small portion of the gold supply need be tied up in this way.

Ricardo's arguments against inflation thus recommended as an ultimate prescription that the "active" domestic money supply be reduced. There was little recognition, however, that such a course of action might lead to disastrous consequences for a nation beset with a drastic shortage of funds which were stringently required to carry out emergency spending projects in foreign nations. Much of the increase in the paper money supply provided by the Bank during the early years of the nineteenth century was utilized by the British government to subsidize its armies during the Napoleonic war. A reduction in paper credit at such a time could not be tolerated. Even after the war was over, the Bank of England provided an important prop to the commercial loan market—one that could not be removed very quickly without creating serious consequences for both private and public borrowers. Ricardo only made a small concession to the important function that the Bank played as a "lender of last resort" when he recommended that the paper money supply be reduced "gradually" so that the market would have time to adjust to the new situation. (R.S. Sayers, pp. 85–86.)

What possible motive could Ricardo have had to all but completely disregard the important credit-creating powers of the Bank of England? Could some appeal to self-interest have caused him to overlook this salutary influence of the Bank and emphasize instead the objectionable effects of over-rapid accommodation to loan demand? What was there about continued inflation that could have caused such a strong adverse reaction from Ricardo as a businessman rather than from Ricardo as an economist? Some

years ago, Professor N. Silberling attempted to answer these
questions by suggesting that Ricardo was primarily interested in
the effect of expanded credit on stock prices rather than on earned
income. (*Q.J.E.*, May 1924.) While Ricardo referred time and
time again to the negative effects rising prices would have on
those individuals who lived on fixed incomes, there is a possibility
that he had strong reasons to fear inflation for personal business
reasons.

Silberling pointed out that Ricardo, as a member of the London
Stock Exchange, was intimately involved in the market for government loans, "the principal type of security traded in at this
time" (p. 427). Ricardo was one of a group of "professional
broker-jobbers" who lent money to private speculators for the
purchase of government securities. The group to which Ricardo
belonged took the bear side of the security market for the lower
the prices at which government obligations stood the stronger was
the expectation in favor of a future price rise, and thus the
interest rate that could be extracted from investors in public ·stock
in exchange for margin loans would be increased. The large
supply of credit made available by the Bank of England to the
domestic banking sector while inconvertibility was maintained
created competition between commercial banks and stock-jobbers
for the right to make these profitable loans, however. Commercial
banks were thus interested in purchasing and marketing large
quantities of government bills with the new funds to which they
were given access. The prices of these securities were thus kept ·
relatively high and the interest rate the jobbers could charge was
lowered to a level close to 5%, which was the legal maximum for
bankers. There is no direct evidence that Ricardo specifically
objected to the accommodating influence of the Bank of England
because it caused the profits of the group of businessmen to which
he belonged to fall. The realization that he had strong financial
interests, however, makes one wonder whether Ricardo, on personal grounds alone, could have initially leaned against the wide
and rather lenient lending powers possessed by the Bank under
the paper standard.

This practice of providing an adequate supply of credit to

private commercial banks and simultaneously supporting the market for public loans was regarded as a crucial mission of the Bank
by Ricardo's foes, the anti-bullionists. These writers emphasized
the important role played by the Bank in domestic emergency and
asserted that no limit could be set to the size of the currency
when important national goals were under consideration. But
Ricardo thought otherwise; he believed England could expand its
foreign expenditures without a significantly larger money supply
because the negative balance of payments implied by large over-
seas purchases would be almost instantaneously self-correcting.
An increase in the money supply under these circumstances
would destroy the workings of this automatic mechanism, leading
to a chronic balance of payments deficit, and it would constitute
additional evidence against unilateral control by the Bank of the
paper money supply. (Viner, *Studies*, pp. 138–45.)

There was, however, a basic error in the analysis of balance of
payments equilibrium that Ricardo provided. He neglected the
short run intermediate consequences of movements in economic
variables and emphasized instead the final clear-cut long run results while disregarding the passage of time which must occur
before they were reached. A negative balance of payments would
thus be corrected by a small amount of paper money flowing out
of the country in the form of foreign remittances. The exchange
value of the paper pound would begin to fall, causing a reduction
in the foreign prices of export goods. The production of these
goods would be expanded, more commodities would be exported,
and the balance of payments deficit would be corrected. If the
Bank of England were to interfere with this process of adjustment
by continually increasing the domestic money supply, the foreign
prices of domestic export goods would be prevented from falling
and the correcting mechanism would cease to operate. A continued negative balance of payments would therefore only be
caused by the profit-seeking nature of the Bank directors. (R.S.
Sayers, p. 80.)

The comparative statics analysis described by Ricardo for the
correction of balance-of-payments disequilibrium neglected the
passage of time because the sequence of steps which described the

readjustment process was assumed to occur *automatically* and *immediately*. No consideration was made of the time it takes to expand or make reallocations of resources in the production of manufactured goods suitable for export. The extent to which the prices of these goods must fall before their foreign demand increased sufficiently was also neglected. Ricardo's rejection of the short run production period in his monetary analysis was carefully underlined by Professor Viner:

Ricardo could very rarely interest himself in the immediate and transitory phases of an economic process sufficiently to trace it in detail through its successive stages, and he frequently confined his analysis to the end results, either passing over without mention or even denying the existence of the intermediate stages. . . . [This habit] gave added force to his exposition when he was dealing with the general public, but it enabled more sophisticated critics to expose him to rebuttal often more damaging in appearance than in fact. (Viner, *Studies*, pp. 139–40.)

Even though Ricardo neglected to discuss the short run production period when he investigated the economic effects of monetary policy, he did make important use of a short run analysis in his writings on another important political issue of the day. This was the famous Corn Law debate. It occupied Ricardo's attention from approximately 1811 to 1815 and provided the impetus for his "Essay on Profits" in 1815. This work contained the core of Ricardo's production and distribution theories, which were to be further developed in the *Principles* (1817). It will be worth our while to examine Ricardo's role in this controversy if we are to understand the true nature of these theoretical constructions, some of which are still important in modern economics.

◄ 4 ►

The Short Run Context Implicit in Ricardo's Analysis of the Corn Laws

During the first half of the nineteenth century, British foreign trade in food-grains was regulated by the so-called "Corn Laws." But the Corn Laws date back to 1660. Their initial purpose was to stabilize the price of food grains, but by the early 1800's protection of the grain producers (farmers) and the land owners had become the overriding consideration in their construction.

The Laws themselves consisted of a complex set of provisions calculated to encourage the exportation of corn and to discourage its importation when its domestic price was relatively low, and also to discourage exportation and encourage importation when its domestic price was relatively high. There were several tariff structures during the tenure of the Laws. An example of one such is the Law of 1804:

Wheat per Quarter
Export. Above 54s., prohibited.
   Over 48s. to 54s., export without bounty.
   At or under 48s., export with 5s. bounty.

Import. At or above 66s., 2nd low duty 7½d.
   63s. to under 66s., 1st low duty 3s. 1½d.
   Under 63s., high duty 30s. 3¾d. (C.R. Fay, p.30)

The Corn Laws lasted from 1660 to 1845. During the first 105 years they worked mostly to regulate the export of food grains, while during the last 80 years they served to reduce the domestic demand for grain imports:

From about 1660 to 1765, there usually was a domestic surplus, and the regulation took the form of an export bounty. . . . During the last portion of their reign, however, they worked to regulate the import of foreign grains. . . . Britain thereafter [after 1765] became an importing country, and the bounty, though not repealed, became inconsequential. (W. Grampp, p. 39.)

During this latter period the Laws became more important politically than they had been. This was caused by the growth of the class of landlord-farmers and their demands for protection from the competition of foreign grains.

The issue of protection lost some of its pertinence during the period 1800–1814, however, when England became involved in the Napoleonic War. This conflict provided a natural barrier against imports of wheat and other grains from the continent of Europe. The Law of 1804 did little to support the price of domestic grain because relatively high prices were furnished by the domestic market operating in isolation from the rest of the world:

In no year between 1804 and 1814 was the average price of wheat as low as the point at which the high duty would come into effect. (C.R. Fay, p. 35.)

When the war ended in 1815, however, a new Corn Law was

being considered in Parliament. Ricardo took an active role in the debate when he wrote his "Essay on Profits" in February of 1815. This pamphlet attacked the proposed Law and, from a wider scope, the whole principle of artificial protection for the home agricultural sector. It was also written in part to answer the pro-Corn Law sentiments expressed by Malthus in the pamphlet, "Grounds of an Opinion," published earlier in the same month. Thus, Ricardo and Malthus became clear political rivals, even though many parts of their economic theories were similar.

The new Corn Law was finally passed by Parliament in March of 1815. It embodied most of the Principles approved of by Malthus in that it attempted to keep the profits in agriculture artificially high by making the postwar prices of grain conform to their wartime levels:

This law was defiantly protective, and differed both in principle and spirit from the legislation of the eighteenth century. It sought to fasten on a country at peace the protection furnished by a generation of war. (C.R. Fay, p. 35.)

This Law lasted from 1815 to 1822 and provided:

. . . full freedom of import without any duty when the price [of wheat] was at or above 80s. the quarter, absolute prohibition when the price was below 80s. (C.R. Fay, p. 41.)

Unlike the effect of changes in the money supply on the real sector of the economy, the relationship between variations in the Corn Laws and adjustments in total production were explained by Ricardo to occur most clearly in a short run context. Population was held constant and domestic demand for food grains increased solely because the tariff charged on foreign wheat (set up by the Corn Laws) was raised.

. . . natural impediments resulting from our increasing wealth and prosperity, oblige[s] us to cultivate at a disadvantage our poor lands, if the importation of corn is restricted or prohibited. If we were left to ourselves, unfettered by legislative enactments, we should gradually withdraw our capital from the cultivation of such lands, and import the produce which is at present raised upon them. ("Essay on Profits," *Works*, 4:32.)

This representative statement describes the essence of Ricardo's short run comparative statics analysis of the Corn Laws. The more difficult is the importation of foreign corn, and therefore the lower the fertility of home land which must be cultivated in order to adequately supply the domestic nation's food requirements, then the higher the price of domestic food. The price of food rises as less fertile domestic land is cultivated because more labor (and capital) becomes embodied in equivalent units of the marginal product. In Ricardo's analysis, the most fertile land is cultivated first and subsequently less fertile land is eventually reached, on which the marginal product of labor has fallen. The lower the marginal product of labor, the greater the amount of labor embodied in equivalent output units and the higher the output price according to the "labor cost" theory of value. (*Principles*, in *Works*, 1:112–14.)

Ricardo's short run (Corn-Law) production mechanism may be summarized as follows: Assume the Corn Laws may be represented by a simple tariff mechanism, so that they may continuously be varied in intensity in relation to the domestic (and foreign) sectors.

> Let T = The tariff rate charged on a unit of imported wheat. It is known, and it may vary due to changes in the Corn Laws.
>
> Let p_1 = Domestic price of domestic agricultural output (wheat).
>
> Let p_{1F} = Foreign price of foreign agricultural output (wheat).
>
> Let $p_{1F} + T$ = Domestic price of imported wheat.
>
> Let x_1 = Domestic agricultural output (wheat).
>
> Let x_{1I} = The amount of wheat imported into the domestic economy.

We are concentrating on the agricultural sector of the domestic economy in order (as Ricardo does) to see how it is affected by a tightening (or a loosening) of the tariff structure implied by the Corn Laws. The tariff rate is therefore the independent variable, while all the other variables are dependent on its value, according to the mechanism implied by Ricardo. Let us carefully investigate the equilibrium path involved in this analysis. Ricardo never explicitly undertook this task but it is indirectly implied by much of what he says in both the "Essay" and the *Principles:*

A.   Initial Equilibrium:

$$p_1 = [p_{1F} + T]_I.$$

Both imported and domestic wheat can be sold for the same price in the home economy.

B. $T\uparrow$

C. $(p_{1F} + T)\uparrow$ immediately to $[p_{1F} + T]_1$, because $T\uparrow$. The domestic price of imported wheat has increased while p_1, the domestic price of domestic wheat, is constant.

$$p_1 < [p_{1F} + T]_1.$$

D.   An (instantaneous) *shift* in demand from the foreign to the domestic wheat producing sector takes place. Increased domestic wheat production follows with the next harvest.

$$x_1\uparrow \quad \text{and} \quad x_{1I}\downarrow \text{ an equal amount.}$$

E. $p_1\uparrow$. As more home wheat is produced, less fertile land must be cultivated, causing the labor cost of equivalent units of wheat output to rise. The rate of increase in p_1 is determined by the fertility of domestic farm land.

$$p_1 = q(x_1) \quad \text{and} \quad \frac{dp_1}{dx_1} > 0.$$

F.   Assume:

$$p_{1F} = h(x_{1I}) \quad \text{and} \quad \frac{dp_{1F}}{dx_{1I}} > 0.$$

This is the same qualitative relationship that Ricardo postulated between the price of wheat and the quantity of wheat produced in the domestic sector if we add the simple requirement that the period of production is short enough so that a reduction of domestic wheat imports also corresponds to a reduction in foreign wheat production. If the technology of wheat production is then similar on the domestic and the international markets,

$$x_{1I} \downarrow \Rightarrow p_{1F} \downarrow.$$

G. As long as domestic wheat production expands, the final equilibrium value of p_1 must be higher than its initial value. But, since the initial increase in T is modified somewhat by the subsequent decrease in p_{1F}, the final value of p_1 is not as high as would be the case without the shift in demand between domestic and foreign sectors outlined above.

To summarize:

$$[p_{1F} + T]_I \uparrow \quad \text{to} \quad [p_{1F} + T]_1$$

because of the increase in T. This is not a final equilibrium position, however. Also, $p_{1F} \downarrow$ because there is a shift in existing demand for wheat from the foreign to the domestic sector. The increase in T and the decrease in p_{1F} results in a final equilibrium value for

$$p_1 = [p_{1F} + T]_2$$

which is somewhere in between the initial and the intermediate values described above. Production of wheat in the home economy expands to the point where the diminishing fertility of land causes the price of wheat to rise so it once more becomes equal to the price of wheat imported from abroad.

This is a description of production in a short run context. A comparison of Ricardo's long run production theory with its short run counterpart may be used to clarify this statement. Ricardo's long run analysis of food production describes an economy in which aggregate grain output expands in response to the enlarging demand of a growing population.

After all the fertile land in the immediate neighborhood of the first settlers were cultivated, if capital and population increased, more food would be required, and it could only be procured from land not so advantageously situated. ("Essay," *Works*, 4:13.)

The equilibrium path described in this quotation is a long run version in which the "stationary state" is being approached. There are three complementary independent variables for this discussion; population growth and capital accumulation are two of them, the third is the tariff rate on foreign wheat. When population expands to a large enough degree, a larger supply of domestic wheat will be required to feed the nation, even if only a minimal standard of living is maintained. This can either come from an expansion of home production or an increase in foreign wheat imports. The final source of this new output depends on the tariff structure relative to foreign wheat, as well as the volume of increased agricultural demand. The higher the tariff on foreign wheat, the more likely will the new requirement be filled from increased domestic supplies. Here we have the tariff mechanism complementing Ricardo's typical growth environment to cause more pronounced expansions in national output than would otherwise be possible. But just as these two processes may be combined, they may be easily separated. When this is accomplished, we can see that the tariff mechanism implied by the Corn Laws can be regarded either as complementing or acting independently from the analysis of growth over time.

Separating Ricardo's analysis of the Corn Laws from his analysis of economic growth, one can notice clearly that the former is a short run theory calculated to explain possible variations in domestic production. We explained above how an increase in the tariff rate could lead to an expansion of domestic wheat production. This was caused by the existing demand for wheat being satisfied from the domestic rather than from the

foreign sector. We should add here that, in the short run, an
expansion in the agricultural sector of the economy would lead to
a contraction in the manufacturing sector. Resources must thus be
reallocated in the economy if we regard population growth and
capital accumulation to be constant. Here, we are regarding two
variables that were independent in the long run analysis as merely
exogenously given in the short run discussion. The only independent variable in Ricardo's short run production mechanism is
therefore the tariff rate implied by the Corn Laws.

Ricardo's arguments against the Corn Laws could thus be
clearly applied in the short run production period and could no
longer be open to the criticism that they disregarded the passage
of time. But an analysis of production which could safely disregard the dimension of time should still examine the adjustment
path between the initial and final equilibrium positions of the
economy. It has just been shown that a careful examination of the
intermediate steps involved would have greatly increased the un-
derstanding of how the economy was operating with respect to
the Corn Laws. But Ricardo was too interested in demonstrating
clear-cut results, so he never explicitly described the sequence of
steps involved in the Corn Law mechanism outlined above.

Looking at Ricardo's Corn Law analysis from a modern perspective, however, we should emphasize the importance placed on
comparing what appear to be temporary positions of equilibrium.
Many analyses of the modern economy also rely on equilibrium
models, but they are much more carefully and formally constructed. However, the fairly recent tendency to construct growth
models of the economy can be directly related to those early
attempts by Ricardo to discover how the Corn Laws could affect
the potential of the domestic economy for economic expansion.
For example, we see that Ricardo's formal method for studying
growth has become popular in some forms of modern analysis; his
description of moving equilibrium relied on a mechanism very
similar to what has become known as "comparative statics." This
method is independent of any operational time framework; it
merely seeks to describe successive equilibrium positions of the
economy. The choice of an exogenous parameter (the tariff rate in

the case of the Corn Laws) provides the continuing impetus to income expansion. Such a method may thus be utilized to describe economic growth, but only in the simplest terms, since it does not analyze the expansion path. Modern development economists have recognized this weakness in the method of comparative statics and have decided to replace it with the "dynamic" study of growth. This method attempts to discover the optimal equilibrium path for a growing nation to follow.

Now that we have reviewed the role of the Corn Law controversy in influencing Ricardo's analysis of the growth of production, we can focus on what Ricardo stated in his *Principles* to be the main problem for the study of political economy: The changing distribution of total produce (total income) to the three (social) income classes—the landlords, capitalists, and laborers. (*Principles*, in *Works*, 1:5.) In order to study the distribution of income according to this formula, first the absolute income quantities —rental, profit, and wage rates—had to be examined; then total rent, profit, and wages could be calculated and the changing share of each in total income could be compared. Let us first investigate the theory Ricardo developed to explain the real wage rate. This is a little-noticed portion of the Ricardian analysis because it admits the possibility that Ricardo did not always regard the real wage rate as a long run datum of his system. It will be shown that, rather than remaining at the fabled "subsistence" level, it can fall steadily when inflation continues to occur in the economy.

‹5›

The Real Wage Rate
as a Welfare Measure
in Ricardo's System

The evolution of Ricardo's analytical system shows that his theories of value, profits, and rent were developed before his theory of wages. The theoretical models Ricardo exhibited in the "Essay on Profits" and the *Principles* show the truth of this statement. The theory of wages was neglected in the "Essay"; instead, the theory of value was used to exhibit an inverse relation between profits and rent:

> We will, however, suppose, that no improvements take place in agriculture, and that capital and population advance in the proper proportion, so that the real wages of labor, continue uniformly the same. . . . ("Essay," *Works*, 4:12.)

The actual formulation of Ricardo's wage theory was begun as a result of a modification of the assumption he made in the

"Essay," that an increase in the price of wheat would not affect the price of "other" (manufactured) goods. Less than a month after the publication of the "Essay," we find Ricardo writing to Malthus that the price of manufactured goods would indeed increase with the price of wheat because wheat is one of the "raw materials" required for the production of such goods. (Letter to Malthus dated 9 March 1815, *Works*, 6:179.)

This indecision concerning whether an increase in the price of wheat would cause the price of "other goods" to rise continued in Ricardo's writings for the next few years and still was present when the *Principles* was finally published. It is an important problem for us to analyze because of the complicated nature of Ricardo's institutional wage payments mechanism set up in this major work. The application of this mechanism led to the conclusion that the real wage rate fell when the price of "other goods" rose with the price of wheat, but it remained constant when the price of "other goods" was unaffected. The falling real wage rate was thought by Ricardo to have an adverse effect on the social welfare of the community, the largest part of which was made up of laborers:

These then are the laws by which wages are regulated, and by which the happiness of far the greatest part of every community is governed. (*Principles*, in *Works*, 1:105.)

Ricardo's wage payments mechanism was directly related to the machinery he assumed to be set up in society for the payment of money wages. Specifically, Ricardo assumed that the worker would be compensated by an increase in money wage payments when the price of domestic wheat increased. But this mechanism asserted that the money wage would rise less than in proportion to the rise in the price of wheat. Hence, the wheat wage rate would fall.

Let us examine the money wage mechanism more closely, in order to distinguish "real" from "wheat" wages. The rise in the money wage rate is determined by two factors: a) the rise in the price of domestic wheat; b) the constant sum of money the worker spends for "other things" (manufactured goods). Ricardo asserted that agricultural labor is always paid a money wage rate which is sufficient to purchase a *constant* amount of higher priced wheat (corresponding to the actual consumption of necessities by the laborer) and sufficient to spend the same amount, totally, on manufactured goods (conveniences).* Ricardo therefore assumed that the market mechanism caused the money wage rate to rise with the price of wheat by an amount sufficient only to offset the rise in the price of the wheat component of the consumer's purchases. The expenditure on necessities rose in proportion to the price of wheat, but expenditure on conveniences remained constant. So the money wage rose at a rate less than proportionate to the rise in the price of wheat. As long as the price of manufactured commodities remained constant, the market basket of goods which the average worker could purchase remained the same. The real wage rate was constant while the wheat wage rate fell. But, if the price of manufactured goods was allowed to increase along with the price of wheat (even though there was a greater percent increase in the price of wheat), and the consumer's total money expenditure on manufactured goods remained fixed, then the increased money wage rate could purchase just as much wheat, but not as many manufactured goods. Even if some substitution between the consumption of wheat and manufactured goods occurred, the real wage rate would fall when the wheat wage rate fell.

Ricardo therefore had included in his *Principles* an argument focusing on the wage mechanism to illustrate how the domestic economy could be ill-affected by the Corn Laws. The rapid increases in domestic wheat production necessitated by regulating

*Here, Ricardo was making his anti-Corn-Law argument stronger by assuming a favorable increase in the money wage rate in response to a higher price of wheat. "The institutional mechanism," he seemed to be saying, "can do no more for workers than prevent the amount of necessities they consume from falling. This may even be too much to expect, but let us make the assumption and see how workers are affected. If they are adversely affected (by a decreasing real wage rate), even under these favorable circumstances, then we should realize that a sudden expansion of domestic wheat output would surely cause many undesirable social problems."

wheat imports could cause the real wage rate to fall. This meant that social welfare would be falling. Unfortunately, as we just demonstrated, Ricardo was indecisive about whether the real wage rate would fall or remain constant when farm output was expanding. The price of manufactured goods would have to rise with the price of wheat in order for the real wage rate to fall. This qualification compromised the effectiveness of the real wage rate as a welfare measure for the economy.

Ricardo thought he had once and for all solved the problem of illustrating the welfare effects of the Corn Laws by including another measure in the *Principles* carried over directly from his "Essay on Profits." He attempted to illustrate how an increase in the money wage rate, as a consequence of the expansion of domestic wheat output, would cause a uniformly falling profit rate. Thus, the profit rate was finally introduced to show how the Corn Laws could be harmful. But this welfare measure, rather than reinforcing the alternative wage mechanism, partially neutralized it because it could operate satisfactorily even if the real wage rate remained constant. The profit rate could fall uniformly throughout the economy only if the price of manufactured goods remained constant when the price of wheat rose. Ricardo seemed to be worried that if both the price of food and the price of finished goods were allowed to rise (and the real wage fall) the profit rate might appear to be falling more slowly in the manufacturing than in the farm sector. (*Principles*, in *Works*, 1:110–11.)

Ricardo's inability to decide definitely on a welfare measure to evaluate growth in the economy thus caused him to offer two measures in his major work which could be used interchangeably. He probably never realized that these two measures had become competing alternatives. After all, both of them justified his point of view that the expansion of domestic agricultural production should be slowed down by a stringent weakening of the Corn Laws to make the importation of food-grains considerably less costly.

‹ 6 ›

The Basic Framework of Ricardo's Production and Distribution Theories

We are now in a position to investigate more closely Ricardo's propositions about how goods are produced in a capitalist society and distributed to its various social classes. These important components of the Ricardian system were discussed in the *Principles* in conjunction with a rather complicated numerical example. This illustration occupied parts of three critical chapters: the last footnote of the chapter on rents (Chapter 2) and considerable portions of the chapters on wages and profits (Chapters 5 and 6). It examined a peculiarly simple economy; a primitive farming community in which labor produced only food grains on various grades of land. It was constructed to analyze the connection between agricultural and general economic growth. The reader's attention was concentrated on the effect of a rising price of grain as its production increased in the domestic economy. The socio-economic community was divided into three

classes: workers, landlords, and capitalists, and the changing relative position of each was evaluated as the economy expanded. The
manufacturing sector was neglected by the example in order to
simplify the derivation of clear-cut results. Furthermore, this sector employed fewer laborers and Ricardo believed that economic
rent was not produced by industry. Therefore, he thought the
important principles of rent could only be examined by analyzing
the farm sector. The principles of wages and profits could be
determined by observing production in either sector of the
economy, and whatever was discovered regarding these quantities
by applying one's efforts to the production of food would
generalize if applied to the economy as a whole. This was the
implicit justification utilized by Ricardo for focusing on agriculture to illustrate his basic principles.

The trends in production and distribution illustrated by the
numerical example depended, once more, on the assumption of an
expanding farm sector throughout which prices were rising and
which was generating this inflationary trend throughout the
economy because the money wage rate was somehow connected
to the price of food. (See Chapter 5 above.) These trends would
be established quite rapidly if a restrictive Corn Law and a strong
demand for wheat were coincident in the domestic economy. This
was the basic short run argument of the "Essay on Profits," which
was written in the heat of the Corn Law debates (late 1814 to
early 1815). The same results would be established much more
gradually, however, if the market for farm goods were expanding
with the natural growth of population. This latter description of
production was more like the basic approach followed in the
Principles. It was a long run argument which tended to neglect the
effect of the Corn Laws. After all, the new Corn Law had already
been accepted by Parliament, and was operative, when Ricardo
wrote the *Principles*. It should be remembered, however, that
Ricardo's anti-Corn-Law policy recommendation provided the initial impetus for the formulation of most of his theoretical production system.

The main difficulty which stands in the path of a clear under-
standing of Ricardo's theorems regarding the distribution of in-

come is the dual nature of the explanation he provided. A significant although minor portion of his effort was spent in describing the changing distribution pattern of a fixed segment of total income allotted to a representative cross section of society. (See H. Barkai, "Ricardo on Factor Prices," pp. 248–49.) The major portion of his analysis, however, was devoted to examining the allocation to society as a whole of growing total income. Ricardo never explicitly recognized this difficulty because each of these analyses yielded the same qualitative results for movements in the distributive shares. But this unusual approach created some confusion in his exposition which the average reader would find difficult to resolve unless it is specifically acknowledged that there are two methods for describing income allocation.*

Table 1 illustrates Ricardo's first approach to the analysis of distributive shares. Columns 1 and 2 indicate that wheat output was produced in response to the application of "doses" of capital/labor to land. Labor was first applied to the most fertile or primary grade land, and then it moved to successively less fertile land as the older land became "filled up." Ricardo realized that time varied as farm production expanded—the rapidity of the pace was determined by the choice of an independent variable —either the tariff on foreign wheat or population growth (see above). One and only one dose of ten laborers with appropriate complementary capital was applied to each grade of land, so that marginal (and average) productivity of the variable input declined as acreage under cultivation increased. Table 1 illustrates that the initial grade of land produced 180 quarters of wheat when one dose of capital/labor was applied to it.

The critical characteristic of this approach to distribution is that Ricardo continued to analyze how the constant produce of only the original land was allocated to society as time progressed. He considered how the total product of 180 quarters of wheat produced on this land was divided among the three classes of society as production was extended onto land of lesser fertility. He ne-

---

*Mr. Barkai, in the article just referenced, did not notice the second method and criticized Ricardo for leaving it out. I believe that Ricardo did indirectly consider "growing total income" when he investigated distribution.

Table 1. *RICARDO'S NUMERICAL EXAMPLE**†

1	2	3	4	5	6
Time sequence. (One dose of the capital/labor input is applied continuously to primary grade land.)	Total wheat product on the first portion of land, minus total wheat rent paid by this land. (The total product is always fixed at 180 units of wheat.)	Price of wheat per unit. ($£$/s/d)	The money value of wheat in the average consumer's market basket. $3 \cdot c3$	The money value of "other things" in the average consumer's market basket.	The money wage rate. $c4 + c5$
1	180	4.0.0	12.0.0	12.0.0	24.0.0
2	170	4.4.8	12.14.0	12.0.0	24.14.0
3	160	4.10.0	13.10.0	12.0.0	25.10.0
4	150	4.16.0	14.8.6	12.0.0	26.8.0
5	140	5.2.10	15.8.6	12.0.0	27.8.6

7	8	9	10	11	12
Total wheat wages paid by the first portion of land. $10 \cdot c6/c3$	The share of total wheat wages in the constant produce of the first portion of land. $c7/180$	Total wheat profits paid by the first portion of land. $c2 - c7$	The share of total wheat profits in the constant produce of the first portion of land. $c9/180$	Total wheat rents paid by the first portion of land. $180 - c2$	The share of total wheat rent in the constant produce paid by the first portion of land. $c11/180$
60.	0.333	120.	0.666	—	—
58.3	0.323	111.7	0.622	10	0.055
56.6	0.314	103.4	0.586	20	0.111
55.	0.301	95.	0.529	30	0.170
53.3	0.298	86.7	0.492	40	0.220

*The collection of the numerical data in this Table, but not the column headings, is given by H. Barkai, "Ricardo on Factor Prices," pp. 247–248. The original source is Ricardo's *Principles*, Chapters on Wages and Profits (Chapters 5 and 6).

†The letter "c" used in the formulas means "column"; e.g., c3 means column 3 of the table.

glected to concern himself explicity with the product of other (less fertile) grades of land, even though they represented most of the total acreage. His task was to explain how a certain quantity of wheat, produced only on a particular grade of "intra-marginal" land, was doled out to the members of society as production expanded and the "extensive" margin of cultivation shifted outwards.

Table 1 does not indicate, and Ricardo never precisely mentioned the nature of "capital" and what proportion of this input was necessary for producing wheat on each grade of land. His chapter on rent in the *Principles* (Chapter 2) did assert, however, that during the process of production rent was formed by the application of "equal" quantities of capital and labor, each to a different grade of land. Each grade of land described in the numerical example had one dose of labor applied to its cultivation, so an "equal" quantity of capital and labor applied to each portion would have to mean that labor and capital were applied to production in *fixed proportions*. That is: The amount of capital combined with a given amount of labor and applied to each different grade of land cultivated would have to be fixed. Land was utilized in the following manner: Initially, grade 1 land was cultivated by one dose of capital/labor. As output increased, a second unit consisting of an identical amount of grade 2 land came into use, being worked by an equivalent dose of capital/labor. Land was never utilized unless it had one uniform dose of capital/labor, and only one, applied to it. The fixed proportion input dose might thus be expanded to include land as well as capital/labor.

The movement of agricultural production onto grades of lesser fertility land caused the product which could be produced to fall. The land of lowest fertility to be cultivated at any time has been called "marginal" land. The progression of cultivation from "intra-marginal" to "marginal" land just described has been called the movement toward the "extensive" margin.

Some economists have noticed another margin in Ricardo's production mechanism which they have called the "intensive" margin. The movement to the intensive margin would occur when more than one dose of capital/labor was applied to intra-marginal land and diminishing returns caused the marginal product of successive doses to fall until it reached the level which was attributed to marginal land. A consistent application of the "intensive" margin to Ricardo's production mechanism would mean that doses of capital/labor were applied to every grade of intra-marginal land until this condition held. (See M. Blaug, *Economic Theory in Retrospect*, p. 83.) But Ricardo only vaguely hinted at the establishment of such an equilibrium condition in his *Principles* or any of his major works. Most of his exposition was instead devoted to describing how land of differing qualities caused certain predictable trends in the distributive shares when total land use was growing.

There is still one open question regarding the nature of production, however, which is related to the heterogeneous character of the capital input. Ricardo, in fact, recognized that there were two types of capital—circulating and fixed—represented in the production process. He thought that the circulating capital fund would only be useful to pay the wages of labor. It turned over quite rapidly in that it was produced during one harvest, consumed as an input to future production, and replenished during the next harvest. Fixed capital, on the other hand, consisted mainly of "buildings and implements." Unfortunately, Ricardo made no explicit mention of fixed capital costs in the *Principles*' numerical example. Therefore, the proportion that existed between fixed and circulating capital during production was also neglected. Even though Ricardo recognized that capital, unlike labor, was heterogeneous, he did not think it important to emphasize this unique characteristic. He must have been making the implicit assumption that the fixed capital stock was being operated at less than full capacity, at least in the farm sector of the economy, so that it did not vary when wheat production was increasing. Therefore "variable" capital consisted only of its circulating component and it could change significantly even in the short run production period. The "capital" component of the fixed proportion capital/labor input dose consisted exclusively of circulating capital.

Table 2 illustrates the second approach to the analysis of distributive shares. Instead of emphasizing how the produce of only

Table 2. RICARDO'S NUMERICAL EXAMPLE (continued)

1	2	3	4*	5
Doses of capital/labor applied to production (10 workers per dose).	The marginal product (MP) of labor on land of various fertilities.	The total product (TP) in wheat produced on all the land placed under cultivation by the corresponding number of variable inputs.	Price of wheat per unit produced. ($£$/s/d)	The money value of wheat in the average consumer's market basket.† $3 \cdot c4$
1/2	180	91.25	4.0.0	12.0.0
1	175	180.		
3/2	170	266.25	4.4.8	12.14.0
2	165	350.		
5/2	160	431.25	4.10.0	13.10.0
3	155	510.		
7/2	150	586.25	4.16.0	14.8.6
4	145	660.		
9/2	140	731.25	5.2.10	15.8.6
5	135	800.		

6	7	8	9	10
The money value of other things in the average consumer's market basket.	The money wage rate. $c5 + c6$	The wheat wage rate. $c7/c4$	Total wheat wages paid by all the land placed under cultivation. $10 \cdot c1 \cdot c7/c4$	The share of total wheat wages in the varying produce of all the land cultivated. $c9/c3$

12.0.0	24.0.0	30.0	6.0	.3288
12.0.0	24.14.0	87.45	5.83	.3286
12.0.0	25.10.5	141.5	5.66	.3285
12.0.0	26.8.0	192.7	5.50	.3284
12.0.0	27.8.6	239.9	5.33	.3282

11	12	13	14
Total wheat rents paid by all the land placed under cultivation. c3 − (c1 · c2)	The share of total wheat rents in the varying produce of all the land cultivated. c11/c3	Total wheat profits paid by all the land placed under cultivation.	The share of total wheat profits in the varying produce of all the land cultivated. c13/c3
1.25	.014	60.	.657
5.			
11.25	.043	167.6	.628
20.			
31.25	.074	258.4	.600
45.			
61.25	.104	332.5	.567
80.			
101.25	.138	390.0	.533
125.			

*In columns 4-10 and 12-14, data is given corresponding to the odd row entries in columns 1-3 only.
†As in Table 1, "c" means "column."

original land is allocated to society as time progresses, this approach examines the allocation of the produce of all grades of land. "Total" product rather than a "partial" representative quantity is described by this discussion. Ricardo believed that the "partial" analysis described earlier could be generalized to hold for the entire economy. Even though in the first instance he clearly intended his Principles' numerical example to explain only how a *fixed* output on a certain grade of land was distributed to the owners of the factors of production, his ultimate goal was to determine how "the proportions of the *whole* produce of the earth" would be so distributed. He must have thought that the distribution trends shown in the case of a fixed output would also hold in the case of a growing output.

The implicit assumption was that the distribution pattern of the fixed wheat product on the second portion of land (170 quarters of wheat) would exhibit the same trends as that of the first portion of land. The same would hold on the third portion of land. Since the whole produce of agriculture was merely the sum of its parts, Ricardo thought that any predictions about distributive shares derived from examining a fixed quality of land would also apply to the complete product of agriculture. It should be emphasized that Ricardo himself never actually computed the total product generated in agriculture (illustrated by column 3) because he was so sure that this generalizing principle would hold. But the partial analysis he did present allows us to make the additional calculations rather easily. We can then examine more closely the production function which he specified and see how the theorems on the distributive shares can be derived.

Table 2, column 1, is labeled, "Doses of capital/labor applied to production," since the capital/labor dose is a variable when we are examining total product rather than only a representative portion of it (compare with Table 1, column 1.). It should be remembered that each new dose of ten laborers is applied to a different grade of land, in an order of decreasing fertility. The entries in the odd rows of Table 2, column 2, are taken from pp. 113–14 of Ricardo's *Principles*. They are considered to be the *total* produce of one dose of capital/labor on each new portion of land. They can also be regarded, however, as marginal products if we assume that the marginal produce decreases as a dose of the variable input is continuously applied to first grade land, having as its average value the entry in the first row of column 2. The marginal product continues to decline on this quality land as is illustrated in row 2, column 2. Rows 1 and 2 of column 2 form a unit. They represent the behavior of the marginal product attributed to the variable input on land of the first quality, while the total product on this land increases from 0 to 180 quarters of wheat. (See Diagram 1.) Each subsequent pair of rows in column 2 represents the behavior of the marginal product of an additional input dose applied to land of the next quality, while total product on each quality of land increases from zero to the value indicated in the odd row of the pair. Notice that the marginal product declines by

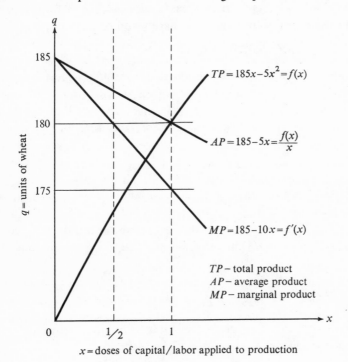

$TP = 185x - 5x^2 = f(x)$

$AP = 185 - 5x = \dfrac{f(x)}{x}$

$MP = 185 - 10x = f'(x)$

TP – total product
AP – average product
MP – marginal product

x = doses of capital/labor applied to production

q = units of wheat

DIAGRAM 1

a constant amount of 10 quarters of wheat from any odd row entry to the next following. Thus, the marginal product schedule is represented by a downward-sloping straight line, as shown in Diagram 1. Units of capital/labor applied to agricultural production are represented on the horizontal axis and units of wheat product are represented on the vertical axis.

Let us see how the total product curve can be derived. The *total* produce of the first portion of land is 180 quarters of wheat. Since one dose of the variable input must be applied to this land, the *average* produce attributed to this input is also 180 quarters when only land of the first fertility is cultivated. Since the marginal product line is downward sloping, it must lie below the average product line at all points other than the zero output level, as is shown in Diagram 1. Therefore, the marginal product must equal 180 quarters of wheat when *less than* one dose of the variable input is applied to production. I have assumed that

$$MP = 180 \quad \text{when} \quad x = \tfrac{1}{2}.$$

Because of Ricardo's assumption that the *MP* line declines at a constant rate of 10 quarters of wheat per dose of the variable input applied, *MP* must be 185 when $x = 0$. We have now determined one point and the slope of the *MP* line, so we can specify its equation:

$$MP = 185 - 10x = f'(x).$$

The even row entries of Table 2, column 2, are calculated by using this equation.

The equation of the total product curve on the diagram corresponding to this *MP* line may now be derived by integration:

$$TP = f(x) = \int f'(x)dx.$$

$$TP = \int (185 - 10x)dx = 185x - 5x^2 + C = f(x)$$

We used the data given by Ricardo to fill in the even row entries of Table 2, column 3. The total product of 3 doses of capital/labor, for example, is the total produce of the first three qualities of land placed under cultivation. (180 + 170 + 160

= 510.) Using the even row entries of column 3, we may calculate the value of C, the constant in the equation for TP:

$$TP = 350, \quad \text{when} \quad x = 2$$
$$350 = 185(2) - 5(2)^2 + C$$
$$c = 350 + 20 - 370 = 0$$
$$TP = 510, \quad \text{when} \quad x = 3$$
$$510 = 185(3) - 5(3)^2 + C$$
$$C = 510 + 45 - 555 = 0$$

C clearly $= 0$

The odd row entries in column 3 are calculated by using the equation just derived:

$$TP = 185x - 5x^2 \cdot (x = 1/2, \ 3/2, \ 5/2, \ 7/2, \ 9/2.)$$

Average product

$$(AP) = \frac{TP}{x} = \frac{f(x)}{x} = 185 - 5x,$$

as is shown in Diagram 1.

We should now turn to a discussion of Ricardo's predictions regarding trends in income distribution which are described by the numerical example summarized in Tables 1 and 2. The conclusions of this practical illustration were supposed to convey an important message about future movements in relative income quantities: Any phenomenon in the economy which contributed to a rise in the price of food grains (expansion of domestic farm output, for example) discriminated in favor of the landlord class and against the farmers (capitalists) and workers. In other words, Ricardo's evaluation of the allocation of a growing total income to the three major social classes was that the share of the landlord class would rise and the shares of the laboring and capitalist class would fall. Let us first examine the wage share of income in order to see how Ricardo derived this interesting result about economic welfare.

‹ 7 ›

Predictions on Changes in Distributive Shares

A. THE WAGE SHARE

Ricardo's proposition that the share of wages in total income would fall was expressed as follows:

We have shown, too, that although the [money] value of the labourer's portion [of the produce of the earth] will be increased by the high value of food [consequent on extending wheat production to less fertile grades of domestic land] his real share will be diminished; whilst that of the landlord will not only be raised in [money] value, but will also be increased in [proportionate] quantity. *(Principles*, in *Works*, 1:112.)

Ricardo, in fact, believed that the theory illustrated by the numerical example confirmed the result that the "real" share of wages in growing total income would fall. But, unfortunately, Ricardo never explicitly calculated the "real" wage rate. Instead, the money wage rate was calculated first using the peculiarly complicated money wage mechanism described above. (See Table 1, columns 3–6, and Table 2, columns 4–7.) Then it was divided by the price of wheat. The "wheat" wage rate thus derived was multiplied by the number of laborers and divided by total income. The result was the share of "wheat" wages in total income rather than the share of "real" wages in total income. It is this "wheat" share which is falling in Table 1, column 8, and Table 2, column 10. This result could not be generalized to the share of "real" wages unless it were known that the "real" wage rate was falling as the "wheat" wage rate fell. We showed above that Ricardo had constructed a mechanism for a falling real wage rate. Unfortunately, he never related this mechanism directly to the numerical example, but in order for his proposition regarding a falling real wage share to hold, it should be so applied.

Table 1, column 8 was calculated as follows: First the price of wheat was calculated. It rose uniformly in the economy as represented by column 3 because in each subsequent time period, the variable input was extended onto less fertile land. This caused its marginal product to fall and the price of wheat to rise because more labor was contained in the final product. (For example: £ 4.4.8 = (180/170) £ 4.0.0. The price of wheat was initially assumed to be £ 4.0.0. The marginal product (*MP*) of the variable input declined from 180 quarters of wheat on primary grade land to 170 quarters of wheat on secondary grade land.) The money value of wheat in the laborer's market basket rose because it was assumed he constantly consumed 3 quarters in column 4. This rising quantity, added to the constant money expenditure on "other things" represented by column 5, illustrates a rising money wage rate in column 6. Column 7 calculates the wheat wage rate, defined as the money wage rate divided by the price of wheat. Table 2, column 10 is calculated in much the same manner as Table 1, column 8.

Comparing Table 1, column 8, with Table 2, column 10, we notice that the wage share decreases about 50 times more quickly when the constant produce of only primary grade land is examined in Table 1 than when total produce is analyzed in Table 2. Here is an example of an income share behaving much differently with regard to the total produce of the economy than it does with regard to a separate portion of that produce. Ricardo never explicitly calculated the "total" relationships shown in Table 2 but as we mentioned above he assumed that the "partial" analysis presented in Table 1 would generalize when it was applied to the entire economy. But now we can see that for the wage share this premise holds only in a qualitative sense. The quantitative rate of decrease in this income share turns out to be much slower when the total production function is finally considered. In order to illustrate why the numbers in Table 2, column 10, decline so slowly, we can construct the equation for total wheat wages described in Table 2 and compare it to the specific production function derived above.

From Table 2, column 9, we can express total wages as:

$$(TWW) = \frac{10 \cdot c1 \cdot c7}{c4} = \frac{10 \cdot c1 \, (c5 + c6)}{c4}.$$

Since column 1 refers to the doses of the variable input injected into the production process, we can let "x" stand for the entries in column 1. Column 5 can then be expressed in money terms as:

$$3\left(\frac{180}{f'(x)} \cdot 4\right).$$

Column 6 = 12, a constant.

$$\text{Column 4} = \frac{c5}{3} = \left(\frac{180}{f'(x)} \cdot 4\right).$$

Therefore:

$$TWW = \frac{10x \left[3\left(\frac{180}{f'(x)} \cdot 4\right) + 12 \right]}{\left(\frac{180}{f'(x)} \cdot 4\right)}$$

$$= \frac{120x \left[180 + f'(x)\right]}{4 \cdot 180}$$

We saw above that:

$$f'(x) = 185 - 10x \quad \text{and} \quad \frac{f(x)}{x} = 185 - 5x.$$

So:

$$f'(x) = 2\frac{f(x)}{x} - 185.$$

Substituting this last expression for $f'(x)$ into Table 2, column 9, we get:

$$TWW = \frac{120x\left[2\frac{f(x)}{x} - 5\right]}{720} = \left(\frac{240}{720}\right)f(x) - \frac{600}{720}x$$

$$= \frac{f(x)}{3} - \frac{5}{6}x.$$

Substituting

$$TP = f(x) = 185x - 5x^2$$

into the expression for

$$\frac{TWW}{TP},$$

we get:

$$\frac{TWW}{TP} = \frac{1}{3} - \frac{5}{6(185 - 5x)}, \quad x < \frac{185}{5}.$$

This last expression is the ratio calculated in Table 2, column 10. Its first derivative is negative. The denominator of the fraction

$$\frac{5}{6(185 - 5x)}$$

is so great compared to its numerator, however, that the rate of decrease in the wage share is the small absolute value illustrated. Ricardo did not realize that his linear production relationship would generalize so poorly and that the importance of the wage ratio as the critical welfare measure for the entire economy would therefore be called into question. For Ricardo realized that the working class was by far the largest class in society, hence one of his strongest and most persuasive arguments aginst the sudden expansion of domestic agriculture was that the relative position of laborers would deteriorate quickly. Any policy which made this class worse off would therefore cause society as a whole to suffer. A more careful examination of Ricardo's numerical example, however, reduces the full force of his predictions regarding the worsening position of the laboring class. Not only does the "total" wage share behave differently from the "partial" wage share, but the "wheat" wage share actually calculated cannot be assumed to behave exactly as would the "real" wage share.

Now that we have found Ricardo's analysis of the wage share to be somewhat weakened, let us turn to his analysis of rents. He predicted that the rental share would be the only one to rise as income expanded in the economy. Therefore, the only class of society to be helped by a rising price of wheat would be the landlord class, the smallest (and the richest) segment of society.

B. THE RENTAL SHARE

Let us first examine the entries in Table 1, columns 2 and 11, to see how rent is formed only on primary grade land. Ricardo described the formation of rent on land of this grade by subtracting the different marginal products of the variable input on lands of lesser fertilities from 180 quarters of wheat, the produce of a uniform dose of the input on primary land. Since land of the second grade yielded a marginal produce of 170 quarters of wheat, total wheat rent on the first grade land increased from 0 to 10 quarters of wheat when production was first expanded. Since the marginal produce of the variable input on land of the third grade diminished to 160 units of wheat as production was further extended, total rent on land of the first grade further increased to 20 units of wheat, and so on.

Why is total wheat rent on the first portion of land calculated in this manner? This was done so that the wheat profit rate stayed uniform throughout the farm sector of the economy. Ricardo was describing a situation in which equal doses of the variable input were applied to equal amounts of land of differing fertilities. The "cost of production" was then the same on all qualities of land because the cost of land itself was considered to be zero. (This was because Ricardo thought arable land had no use other than to grow crops. See Blaug, *Economic Theory*, p. 84.) The produce was 180 units of wheat on land of the first quality and 170 units on land of the second quality. As long as the farmer of the first portion of land was allowed to retain the 10 unit differential between the two outputs, it would be profitable for farmers of second grade land, or new farmers, to begin cultivating first grade land until diminishing marginal productivity on this land removed the differential. In other words, the wheat rate of profits was higher on first grade land than it was on second grade land as long as a differential existed between the marginal products on these land qualities. In equilibrium, the wheat rate of profits was to be equalized on all qualities of land. Therefore, landlords could charge 10 units of wheat rent on the first grade of land when the second grade of land was marginal, so that no differential would exist in the return to the farmer on either grade of land. Rent increased similarly on primary land as production continued to be extended. (See Table 1, columns 2 and 11.)

This description of the formation of rent indicated that the agricultural profit rate was determined by the productivity of marginal land. Furthermore, the profit rate fell uniformly as land of lesser fertility was placed under cultivation. As Ricardo said: ". . . the rate of . . . profits will diminish in proportion to the rise in the price of corn." (*Principles*, in *Works*, 1:113.) This uniformity of the profit rate was brought about when the net return to intramarginal farmers (after rent was paid) was equated to the return to the farmer of marginal (no-rent) land. Now that we have examined the formation of rent on only primary grade land, we are in a position to calculate total rent in the entire farm sector of the economy. We shall have to add together the individual rent components associated with each grade of land in order to accomplish our purpose. Ricardo never explicitly undertook this task, but we shall see that a general formula for rent can be derived by specifically summing up these separate rent quantities.

We can use the marginal product schedule constructed in Table 2, column 2, to derive total wheat rent on all qualities of land. First we calculate rent on first quality land, then we calculate rent on lesser fertility grades of land subsequently cultivated, and finally we sum up these figures. Let the last grade of land to be cultivated (marginal land) be fifth quality land. (See Diagram 2.) We know that total wheat product (q) = the area under the MP line ZP. (This is the same MP line as was drawn in Diagram 1.) The total wheat produce of only fifth quality land is then the area

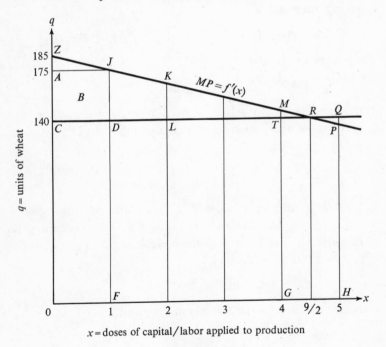

DIAGRAM 2

of *MPHG*. This area = 140 according to the numerical example. Furthermore, *MPHG* = *TQHG* = 140, since triangle *TMR* is congruent to triangle *RQP*. The total product of only first quality land equals triangle A + rectangle B + *CDFO* = 180 = *ZJFO*. *CDFO* = 140 = *TQHG*, the total produce of only fifth quality land. Total wheat rent associated with first quality land when marginal land is of the fifth quality equals the difference between the produce of one dose of the variable input on these two land grades.* *ZJFO* − *CDFO* = *ZJDC* = 40. The total wheat rent on the second portion of land, when the margin of cultivation is land of the fifth portion, is similarly *JKLD*. Therefore, in order to calculate total wheat rent in the entire farm sector, we need to know the margin of cultivation; then we can sum up the total rents associated with each grade of land. This summation process gives, in the limit, an area in Diagram 2 represented by the following integral:

$$\text{Total Wheat Rent} = TWR = \int_{o}^{x_0} f'(x) - f'(x_0)dx.$$

The integration yields:

$$TWR = f(x_0) - x_0 f'(x_0).$$

The symbol x_0 is an arbitrary fixed point, corresponding to a certain level of application for the variable input. In Diagram 2,

$$x_0 = \frac{9}{2},$$

and *TWR* = area of triangle *ZRC*. The area of integration is bounded by the *MP* line and the horizontal line representing the marginal product of x_0 units of the variable input. The calculation of rent in Table 2, column 11:

$$c3 - (c1 \cdot c2),$$

is exactly the same as the formula just derived.

$$x_0 = \frac{1}{2}, \ 1\frac{3}{2}, \ 2\frac{5}{2}, \ 3\frac{7}{2}, \ 4\frac{9}{2}, \ 5.$$

---

*This condition must hold in order to equilibrate the profit rates on land qualities one and five as was described above.

Table 2, column 12 shows the various shares of rent in total product. The ratio increases as production expands. Using algebra we can see why.

$$\frac{TWR}{TP} = \frac{f(x) - xf'(x)}{f(x)} = \frac{(185x - 5x^2) - x(185 - 10x)}{185x - 5x^2}$$

$$= \frac{5}{-5 + \dfrac{185}{x}}$$

$$\left(0 < x < \frac{185}{5} \right)$$

This algebraic formula is another representation of the entries in Table 2, column 12. The first derivative of this ratio is clearly positive. Comparing Table 1, column 12, with Table 2, column 12 we can see that the rent share increases at a very similar rate either when the produce of primary grade land is isolated or when farm produce is examined as a whole. Let us now turn to Ricardo's analysis of profits. As with the wage share, Ricardo thought that the share of profits in total income would decline as production expanded.

C. THE PROFIT SHARE AND THE PROFIT RATE

The calculation of total wheat profits on only primary grade land is illustrated by Table 1, column 9. Profits are regarded as a residual—the difference between the constant produce of 180 and rent plus wages paid on this land as production expands in the economy. Correspondingly, total wheat profits produced in the entire agricultural sector are calculated in Table 2, column 13, utilizing the same basic method. The expression $c3$ represents total wheat product, $c3 - (c1 \cdot c2)$ represents total wheat rents, and

$$\frac{10 \cdot c1 \cdot c7}{c4}$$

represents total wheat wages.

Total Wheat Profits

$$= c3 - \left[c3 - (c1 \cdot c2)\right] - \left(\frac{10 \cdot c1 \cdot c7}{c4}\right)$$

$$= c1 \cdot c2 - \frac{10 \cdot c1 \cdot c7}{c4}.$$

The fraction shown to the right above is total wheat wages *(TWW)*; the entries for c1 (column 1) represent doses of the variable input and have been represented previously by "*x*"; the entries for c2 (column 2) represent marginal product *(MP)* and have been represented previously by "*f′(x)*." We showed previously that:

$$TWW = \frac{f(x)}{3} - \frac{5}{6}x.$$

Therefore, the share of total wheat profits *(TWP)* in total product can be expressed as follows:

$$\frac{TWP}{TP} = \frac{xf'(x)}{f(x)} + \frac{5x}{6f(x)} - \frac{1}{3}.$$

Utilizing the expression derived above,

$$f'(x) = 2\ \frac{f(x)}{x} - 185,$$

we can simplify this ratio:

$$\frac{TWP}{TP} = \frac{5}{3} - \frac{1105}{6}\ \frac{x}{f(x)}.$$

The fraction $x/f(x)$ is the reciprocal of average product and it increases when farm production expands because average product falls. *TWP/TP* therefore decreases. This ratio is calculated in Table 2, column 14. The rate of decrease in the entries of this column is about ¾ as great as the rate of decrease of the entries in Table 1, column 10. This latter column illustrates the changing share of total wheat profits paid by only the first portion of land in constant produce (180 quarters of wheat). This partial analysis of changes in the share paid to farmer-capitalists generalizes quite well when it is applied to the total produce of agriculture.

Now that we have examined total profits, let us to some extent investigate the profit rate. One conclusion of the chapter, "On Profits" (Chapter 6 of Ricardo's *Principles*), was that the profit rate would vary inversely with the money wage rate. Thus, when agricultural production expanded, forcing up the price of wheat and the money wage rate, the rate of profits in the farm sector would fall. This would, in turn, lower the profit rate in the remainder of the economy because of the assumption of perfect mobility of factors referred to above. The prediction of a falling profit rate was one of the main contributions of Ricardian economics to Marxian theory. Therefore, it is well worth observing how this interesting proposition was derived.

Since we will relate the profit rate to the "money" wage rate, we should first calculate total "money" profits *(TMP)*.

$$1. \quad TMP \ = p_1q \ - \ xW_M \ - \ TMR.$$

Let x be the number of standard capital/labor doses applied to farm production. *TMP* is defined as a residual just as it was in Ricardo's numerical example; p_1 = price per unit of wheat output; $q = f(x)$ = total wheat output; p_1q = total money output of agriculture; W_M = money wage rate; xW_M = total money wages paid in agriculture; *TMR* = total money rent. Let *TWR* = total wheat rent.

$$2. \quad TMR \ = p_1(TWR) \ = \ p_1q \ - \ p_1xf'(x),$$

where

$$\frac{dq}{dx} \ = f'(x).$$

(See the definition of *TWR* formulated above in the section on rent.) Substituting 2 into 1, we get:

$$3. \quad TMP \ = p_1xf'(x) \ - \ xW_M$$

Assume that each dose of capital and labor consists of m units of physical capital per one unit of labor. Let v = money profit per unit of capital (the profit rate).

$$4. \quad TMP = mvx$$

Substituting 4 into 3, we get:

$$5. \quad mv = p_1 f'(x) - W_M$$

$$6. \quad p_1 = \frac{a}{f'(x)}, \quad \text{where } \text{``}a\text{''} \text{ is a constant.}$$

This is a statement of the labor theory of value as expressed in the numerical example; $a = (4 \cdot 180) = 720$. (See Table 2, columns 2 and 4.)

Substituting 6 into 5 and taking the derivative of 5 with respect to q, we can see how the profit rate will fall when wheat output is expanding:

$$7. \quad \frac{mdv}{dq} = \frac{-d W_M}{dq} < 0, \quad \text{since } \frac{d W_M}{dq} > 0.$$

(See H. Barkai, "Ricardo's Static Equilibrium," p. 24.)

Ricardo's wage mechanism was carefully constructed to illustrate the rise of the money wage rate with the expansion of domestic farm output. Therefore, the profit rate would fall uniformly throughout the economy as long as the supply of land of any given quality was limited.

Summary

It has been shown that the most important elements of Ricardian economics are composed of a curious blend of political advocacy and detailed analysis of a simplified real-world model. Ricardo normally began his examination of the economy by focusing on one of the current debates such as the Corn Law or bullionist controversies, then, as the issues involved dimmed in importance, he started to examine the underlying elements more closely. His final conclusions regarding these variables were sometimes completely divorced from the practical motivation which initially caused him to begin his investigations. Thus, the profit rate was finally predicted to fall as expansion of the economy continued. But the falling profit rate was originally demonstrated in the "Essay on Profits" as one of the effects of a strong Corn

Law on the domestic economy. Ricardo wanted to make the point that repealing this law would *prevent* the profit rate from falling in the future. When the political issue of the Corn Laws was finally closed, however, his emphasis on how to prevent the profit rate from falling was replaced by a description of how reductions in the profit rate were almost a foregone conclusion. Limiting one's readings to the *Principles*, one would not get the strongly optimistic influence on Ricardo's analysis provided by his recommendation that the Corn Laws be eliminated.

Furthermore, Ricardo's system appeared not to be well integrated because of his extreme shift in emphasis from the money to the output sector in his analysis of the economy. Politics also played a role in this problem area, however. Ricardo's first economic writings concerned the Bullionist controversy and were almost exclusively concerned with problems of regulating the money supply. The later analysis of the Corn Laws, however, illustrated a strong concern with the output market and an almost total neglect of the money market. But we showed above that although the careful analysis of production and distribution begun by Ricardo in the "Essay" and completed in the *Principles* artifically neglected the role of money, the earlier analysis carried out in his monetary pamphlets gave some strong indications that variables in the money and output markets could be simultaneously determined.

This comparison of Ricardo's writings on money with his analysis of production in the real sector revealed that the examination of problems in both these sectors was undertaken by utilizing the concept of "equilibrium." For the money market, equilibrium was described mainly in terms of the "quantity theory." But we noticed that Ricardo's application of the quantity theory was not exclusively a "crude" interpretation in which the money supply determined the price level in isolation from all other production relationships. Conditions in the output market had a definite effect on the general price level. In this way, Ricardo applied the equilibrium concept to both major sectors of the economy in a complementary fashion.

There was a major problem with Ricardo's conception of equilibrium, however, because he neglected to consider carefully the implications of "operational time." Thus, he described long run adjustments as if they took place instantaneously, while he never presented a careful description of the short run production period. This latter period for analysis was seen to be especially important if we wished to accurately describe Ricardo's position against the Corn Laws.

The last part of this study of Ricardo was concerned with describing the method he used to calculate the three major social income shares: wages, rent, and profits. One interesting conclusion from this illustration which has yet to be mentioned is its similarity with the analysis of the more modern marginal productivity theorists. We hinted at a description of "perfect competition" when we discussed how the profit rate was equalized throughout the economy during the formation of rent. The assumptions of "perfect mobility" and "perfect knowledge" were included. Moreover, the section on profits illustrated an equation (number 5) which represents the modern equilibrium condition for profit maximization: The value of marginal product, $p_1 f'(x)$, was set equal to marginal cost, $W_M + mv$ (the wage cost plus the capital cost of extending farm production). This result shows that Ricardo's system has some interesting similarities to more current economics which are not generally noticed.

Of course, there are also many gaps which have been left between Ricardian and neoclassical economics, some of which have been the topic for recent research efforts into the theory of capital. (See G. Harcourt, "Some Cambridge Controversies in the Theory of Capital.") These investigations closely examine the nature of the capital input in a generalized production function, a complicated problem that Ricardo only indirectly attacked in his *Principles*, Chapter 1, "On Value."*

The focus of Ricardo's analysis was agriculture rather than

---

*Ricardo investigated the nature of the capital input when he showed how ". . . different proportions of fixed capital or different durabilities of fixed capital or different times necessary to bring (a commodity) to market . . ." could change the relative value of a good when the money wage rate varied even though the "real" labor cost remained constant. (P. Sraffa, *Works*, 1:xli.) Thus, Ricardo brought capital as well as labor into the value forming process. But he regarded the effect of capital on the system of relative prices to be very small and chose virtually to disregard it as an unimportant exception in the text of the *Principles*.

manufacturing—where labor, rather than capital, was considered the prime factor of production. We can justify his neglect of capital by noting this fact, but it is still interesting to observe the methodology followed by later economists when they carefully compared the Ricardian and the neoclassical systems, taking into account the complexities of this critical input.

Modern writers have been able to show that an amazing correspondence exists between the Ricardian labor cost theory of value and the so-called "neoclassical parables" of distribution theory, the most famous of which are perfect competition and the equilibrium condition that all factors are paid their marginal products (G. Harcourt, pp. 379 and 387). In fact, it can be shown that when only labor is responsible for value determination, these modern results can be derived directly from the value equation.

Some economists had thought that even with a generalized cost-of-production theory of value (in which capital as well as labor was part of the value forming process) this close connection would still exist between objective value determination and the distributional results of the perfectly competitive model. After all, aggregate value determination and distribution theory in the neoclassical system depended on objectively measuring both these inputs (rather than only labor) together with examining the effects of technical change on production in the economy. If the major results concerning distribution could not be derived from the basic cost of production income equations, then there would be a lack of consistency between the elements of modern economics.*

*From the viewpoint of neoclassical economics, "aggregate" income played the same role as "individual" exchange value did in the Ricardian system. Instead of linking individual value with their distributional results, these later economists preferred to focus on total income payments in each sector. Income generated in each sector was then regarded as that sector's contribution to exchange value. Relative value could then be determined by comparing the contribution of each sector. The pattern of income distribution together with the equilibrium results of the "neoclassical parables" should follow from the income equations in order for this system to be logically integrated. If they do not, the idea of aggregate value should possibly be simplified to an exclusively labor concept as it was in Ricardo. (G. Harcourt, equations 3.1 and 3.2, p. 389.)

This is the question to which the "double-switching"* debate addresses itself. Those economists who defend the theories so important in current "Principles" books state that an essential consistency exists between neoclassical value, production, and distribution theory. On the other hand, there are those who think Ricardian economics, even though less formally complete, is a better logical system, because the neoclassical results concerning distribution can be derived quite easily. Furthermore, this latter group holds that these results do not follow from the basic cost-of-production equations of income determination explicitly constructed by the neoclassicists themselves and retained by modern economists. They believe that once double-switching is allowed, the distributional results "disappear" and modern economic theory is left in a vacuum. Whatever the final resolution of this debate, one thing it certainly has accomplished is to emphasize the importance of Ricardo's contributions to the methodology and to the specific subject matter of current economics.

---

*Double-switching is defined as follows: " . . . the same method of production may be the most profitable of a number of methods of production at more than one rate of profit (r) even though other methods are more profitable at values of r in between. . . ." (G. Harcourt, p. 388.)

Appendix: The Intensive Versus the Extensive Margins of Land Cultivation

The difference between the "intensive" and the "extensive" margins when agricultural production expanded in the Ricardian system was mentioned briefly in Chapter 6 above. The movement to the intensive margin was described by successive doses of uniform capital/labor input being applied to intramarginal land until diminishing returns caused the marginal wheat product to fall to the same level that was attributed to marginal land. It was also stated that Ricardo never put specific emphasis on this equilibrium condition. In fact, although one can find passing reference in some of Ricardo's works to the possibilities for increasingly intensive uses of given land qualities, the equalization of marginal wheat product throughout the farm sector was never explicitly stated as a goal of such expanded farm production. We shall show in this appendix, however, that the idea of an intensive margin can be closely related to two other explicitly mentioned characteristics of the Ricardian system: A) the equalization of the profit rate or the uniformity of the profit rate throughout the farm sector, and B) the model of perfect competition that Ricardo was describing.

The movement to the extensive margin occurred when land of a progressively less fertile grade was utilized to produce the expanding farm output. It should be recalled that the Ricardian numerical example described above seemed to illustrate *fixed proportions* between all three basic inputs: capital, labor, and land. (See Chapter 6.) But if we wish to focus on the concept of the extensive margin it will be necessary to treat land as an independently variable input of the system. Therefore, even though the capital/labor dose will continue to be combined in fixed proportions, land will be regarded as a separately determined production variable.

PART 1:   THE INTENSIVE MARGIN

The discussion of the intensive margin can be directly related to the profit mechanism Ricardo utilized. The rate of profits in the farm sector of the Ricardian economy was discussed above in two different contexts. At the end of Chapter 7, we discussed the inverse relationship between the profit rate and the money wage rate. We let "v = money profit per unit of capital (the profit rate)." Earlier in the same chapter, in connection with the description of rent formation, we showed how the profit rate would be equalized on each different grade of farm land by the subtraction of rent from the total produce of the variable input (the fixed proportion dose of capital/labor) on each portion of intramarginal land. But, during this discussion, we neglected to consider the possibility that more than one dose of the input could be applied to land within the external margin. This interesting situation was not always neglected by Ricardo, however. In isolated instances he did consider that capital/labor could vary in relation to a *fixed* total quantity of heterogeneous land. This is what later economists have called the movement to an "intensive" margin. Even though Ricardo did not particularly emphasize this aspect of his production system, it is still worth describing in detail because a connection can be established between such an analysis and Ricardo's ideas concerning perfect competition.

The intensive margin was achieved, once more, by the adjustment of the profit rate throughout agriculture to the rate prevailing on marginal land, utilizing the explicit assumption that the quantity of land was fixed. The total supply of land was further broken up into various qualities suitable for cultivation. As the amount of capital/labor injected into the agricultural production process increased, all the different grades of land previously cultivated were cultivated more "intensively" until the rate of profit was equalized on each grade.

Ricardo described the movement to the "intensive margin" of land cultivation in the following manner:

It often, and, indeed, commonly happens, that before No. 2, 3, 4, or 5, of the inferior lands are cultivated, capital can be employed more productively on those lands which are already in cultivation. It may perhaps be found, that by doubling the original capital employed on No. 1, though the produce will not be doubled, will not be increased by 100 quarters, it may be increased by eighty-five quarters, and that this quantity exceeds what could be obtained by employing the same capital, on land No. 3. (*Principles*, in *Works*, 1:71.)

The least fertile land cultivated in the economy (the marginal land) determined how "hard" every other quality of land must be utilized. Capital/labor was allocated to the fixed supply of each portion of land until the produce of an added unit of this input on each different fertility of land was equal to the produce of one unit on marginal land.* This was the condition which Ricardo

---

*Unfortunately, Ricardo never explicitly stated this final equilibrium condition. It was implied by much of what he wrote, however. It was assumed that the marginal produce of labor diminished on each different quality of land, the same as it did when labor moved to less fertile land. The rate of profit on each grade of intramarginal land was adjusted to the rate of profit prevailing on marginal (no-rent) land by the formation of rent on intramarginal land. (See Chapter 7.)

was hinting at in the last quotation. It was an equilibrium condition. Total farm produce would increase as long as this equality remained unsatisfied, but such produce was at its maximum when there was an equality of the marginal products on each grade of land.

The Ricardian idea of an intensive margin equilibrium, when combined with his analysis of rent, illustrated how profit rates would be equalized in agriculture. But was this profit rate uniformity related to profit maximization throughout the economy? (For our simple model, the total economy consists only of the farm sector.) Can we thus relate Ricardo's theories to this much discussed requirement, which is usually regarded as an equilibrium condition for a "rational" firm?* Furthermore, what role did perfect competition play in the adjustment mechanism described by Ricardo? Did his system so closely approximate this ideal market organization, as is sometimes presumed?

Although Ricardo never stated explicitly that total profits should be maximized in the economy, we can illustrate a consistency between this condition and profit rate uniformity by proving the following theorem:

THEOREM: If profits are maximized throughout the Ricardian full employment farm sector, and if the profit rate on each grade of land is invariant with respect to increased production, the rate of profits must be identical throughout agriculture. (For purposes of simplification, no manufacturing sector exists and the total economy consists exclusively of the farm sector.)

It should be explained what we mean by making the assumption of full employment. In a simple sense it refers to the fact that the supply of the basic capital/labor input equals its demand. But, since earlier we spoke of the effect of the Corn Laws on the production system in a short run context, we can assume more specifically that: A) X_0, the supply of the capital/labor input in the

---

*Maximization of profits in the *entire* agricultural sector corresponds to the theory of the firm equilibrium condition of modern economics, but it is an *aggregate* version of this condition with all the "farm firms" combined into one large firm (the farm sector).

economy is fixed, and B) Ricardo's belief in Say's Law implies that the output market is instantaneously cleared so that employment remains at its high level even with a rather short period of adjustment.

PROOF: Let $\prod$ = total profits in the economy.

Let v_i $(i = 1, \ldots, n)$ = money profit per unit of capital (the profit rate) on each of the n grades of land placed under cultivation.

Let x_i $(i = 1, \ldots, n)$ = the number of units of the fixed proportion capital/labor doses applied to each of the n grades of land placed under cultivation.

Let m = the number of units of physical capital combined with each unit of labor, which makes up the standard input dose.

Then, mv_ix_i $(i = 1, \ldots, n)$ = total money profits generated on each of the n grades of land.

We wish to illustrate a connection between the maximization of total profits and the uniformity of the profit rate. Let us therefore maximize the function:

$$\prod = mv_1x_1 + mv_2x_2 + \ldots + mv_nx_n = f(x_1, \ldots, x_n)$$

subject to the full employment constraint,

$$X_0 = x_1 + x_2 + \ldots + x_n.$$

Form the objective function:

$$Z = mv_1x_1 + mv_2x_2 + \ldots + mv_nx_n + \Lambda (X_0 - x_1 - \ldots - x_n),$$

where Λ is the Lagrange multiplier. Setting the partial derivatives equal to zero, we get the following first order conditions for a maximum:

$$\frac{\partial Z}{\partial x_i} = \left[mv_i + mx_i \frac{\partial v_i}{\partial x_i} \right] - \Lambda = 0 \ (i = 1, \ldots, n),$$

where

$$\frac{\partial \prod}{\partial x_i} = \left[mv_i + mx_i \frac{\partial v_i}{\partial x_i} \right].$$

If we can assume that

$$\frac{\partial v_i}{\partial x_i} = 0,$$

then these n conditions clearly establish that:

$$\Lambda = mv_1 = mv_2 = \ldots = mv_n \quad \text{or} \quad v_1 = v_2 = \ldots = v_n;$$

the profit rates are identical on each grade of land cultivated.

$$\frac{\partial v_i}{\partial x_i} = 0$$

means that the profit rate on each grade of land is invariant with respect to increased production. This assumption can be directly related to the idea of perfect competition. The entire agricultural sector can be thought of as one large industry which can be divided into a number of representative firms. Each firm would operate on a different quality of land.

$$\frac{\partial v_i}{\partial x_i} = 0$$

is then a statement that no one firm can affect the going profit rate. It is a restatement of the famous "no market power" assumption in models of perfect competition. It says that a small increment to the uniform input applied to production by any farm firm cannot affect the rate of profit prevailing in agriculture.* Ricardo never made such an assumption, but we have shown that if he had, his description of the formation of rent by the equalization of profit rates together with his idea of an intensive margin where

*An exact statement of "no market power" would specify that farmers on each quality of land make production decisions independently. Furthermore, the number of farmers would have to be so large and the share of each in total farm production would have to be so small that the variation in wheat output obtained by applying an additional unit of input would not affect the price of wheat in the economy. Presumably, the rate of profit could remain constant even if the price of wheat should vary. Therefore, the assumption that $\partial v_i/\partial x_i = 0$ may not exactly be equivalent to the idea of "no market power."

capital/labor varied in relation to a fixed total quantity of land would have been consistent with the allegedly neoclassical condition of profit maximization.

Ricardo did make the other three assumptions required for perfect competition in one form or another, however. Since he never differentiated between varieties of "corn" in his discussion of agriculture, he must have been dealing with a "homogeneous" product. His discussion of the equalization of the profit rate throughout the economy illustrated the "perfect mobility" of factors between employments. If the profit rate were higher in one line of employment than in another, the application of the variable factor would shift toward its most profitable alternative use. The description of a uniform wage rate for menial labor so evident in the construction of the *Principles'* numerical example discussed above implied that workers possessed "perfect knowledge" of rates of return paid for their services. Therefore, Ricardo's "model" of the economy came close to exhibiting what modern economists have called "perfect competition." The analysis just completed demonstrates how this ideal market mechanism can be related directly to profit maximization, so we can now state that the modern "theory of the firm" owes more to Ricardian theory than has so far been recognized.

PART 2:   THE EXTENSIVE MARGIN

The discussion of the intensive margin just completed illustrates a resultant equilibrium condition as the variable capital/labor input increased in relation to a fixed supply of differing fertility lands. The process of adjustment Ricardo described showed how the profit rate would tend to be equalized on each quality of land. We can now describe the movement to an alternative equilibrium by observing how total wheat product would increase when land varies in relation to a fixed amount of capital/labor. This movement has been referred to in the literature as an adjustment toward the "extensive" margin. We will show that just as Ricardo never accurately and completely described the intensive margin, he also never explicitly stated conditions for an extensive margin. But if we include the assumption of profit maximization as part of the analysis (something Ricardo only hinted at, as we just noted) we can illustrate specifically the relationship of extensive margin equilibrium to the diminishing returns production function Ricardo described for agriculture.

The explanation of the extensive margin can be clarified if we redefine the farm production function as follows: $q = f(x, L)$, where q = total wheat output, x = the number of standard capital/labor doses applied to farm production, and L = the level of land cultivation. The two basic inputs are x and L. Both these inputs should be regarded as independent variables with respect to q. The discussion of Ricardo's numerical example above (in Chapter 6) illustrated a situation in which L seemed to be combined in fixed proportions with x because each succeeding unit of x was applied to a lower quality of land. But the current analysis allows the ratio between x and L to change so that a variable proportions production function is being described. Since the quantity of land cultivated is an independent variable relative to farm output, it helps determine (it is not determined by) the level of production. L is not dependent, as it was in the description of the numerical example, on the quantity of x utilized as an input.

Part 1 of this appendix demonstrated how close Ricardo's production mechanism came to describing profit maximization. Related to this result, we illustrated above at the end of Chapter 7 that as long as the price of the homogeneous wheat output and the profit rate were both uniform in the economy, Ricardo's definition of rent could lead to the now famous optimality condition for hiring factors:

$$(A) \quad p_1 f'(x) = W_M + mv.$$

(See Chapter 7, equation 5.) The marginal revenue product of the capital/labor input was set equal to its marginal cost: the wage cost plus the total cpaital cost of employing the last unit of labor. Since x was the only independent variable in this equation, this condition for profit maximization would hold only for what we have just characterized as the movement to the intensive margin. The movement to the extensive margin can be represented by a separate equation, however, which would be analogous to the above equation in its description of profit maximization, but would also take into account the independent nature of the land input. This equation may be stated as follows:

$$\text{(B)} \quad \frac{\partial q}{\partial L} = 0.$$

The marginal revenue product of the land input should be set equal to its marginal cost, but this is zero for the Ricardian analysis because Ricardo assumed land to be of no use in the production of goods other than wheat. There were no alternatives open to the employment of land other than its use in the cultivation of food. If it were not used in the production of food grains, it would remain idle. This equation states as an equilibrium condition that "free" land is applied to a fixed amount of the capital/labor input until no more wheat product can be produced. We noted above (Chapter 6) that as cultivation proceeded, the most fertile (highest average productivity) land was applied first and then subsequently less fertile grades were applied to wheat production. Therefore, this equilibrium condition means that grades of land of less and less fertility are added to the fixed capital/labor stock until the only land still potentially capable of supporting the growth of food grains is not fertile enough to yield any additional wheat output.

The equilibrium adjustment mechanism described by equation B determines the total amount of land of all fertilities *(L)* which would be utilized in the cultivation of wheat. The size of this variable, together with the assumption that cultivation proceeds on land in order of decreasing fertilities, fixes the fertility of the last land to be cultivated.* The solution for the last land to be cultivated has been called the determination of the "extensive margin" in classical economics.

The following quotation supports our view that land is a free good in the Ricardian system and establishes a connection be-

---

*We must also assume here that the supply of each quality of land is known and fixed.

tween this proposition and the extensive margin in the Ricardian analysis:

The only kind of rent considered in the Ricardian theory is agricultural rent; moreover, it is rent for the "raw produce" of agriculture as a whole, not rent for land devoted to particular products. Land used for tillage is thought to have no competing uses for grazing; labor and capital shift from one unit of land to another, but land itself never shifts between alternative uses. This explains the presence of the extensive margin in classical rent theory: land is supposed to be taken up free when needed, not from some other rent-paying alternative, but from non-paying idleness. (Blaug, *Economic Theory*, pp. 84–85.)

Equation B is one of the conditions for agricultural sector profit maximization, and as such completes the construction of the framework begun by equation A. These two equations together show: (1) How many different qualities of land will be cultivated. (Equation B shows this, since it fixes the quality of the "last" land cultivated.) (2) How much capital/labor will be applied to wheat production on each separate quality of land cultivated. (Equation A shows this, since it asserts that capital/labor is added to each grade of land until the value of the marginal product is equal to its marginal cost.) The marginal cost of capital/labor on every portion of land cultivated is the same and is determined by the uniform wage rate of labor and the uniform profit rate in the economy. It should be noted that equation A was formulated by direct reference to the definition of rent illustrated in Ricardo's numerical example, but equation B could not be explicitly related to his system. Although Ricardo omitted an exact specification of this equation, we have just shown that it should be added to his system if we wish to make the notion of profit maximization symmetric, that is, dependent on both an extensive as well as an intensive margin.

However, Ricardo came close to describing the extensive margin condition contained in equation B when he stated that, during the process of production, ever decreasing fertilities of land (the quantities of which were known and fixed) would be added to the stock of the capital/labor input. This stock would increase at a

constant rate rather than remaining stationary until, as a condition
of long run equilibrium, the rate of profits became so close to zero
that no investment would take place.* There was no special
reason why a close-to-zero rate of profits in the economy should
coincide with the point where the marginal wheat product of land
was zero. Therefore, there was no special reason why the fertility
of the last land to be cultivated, determined by such a long run
method, should be the same as the quality of the marginal land,
determined by the use of equation B. But the usefulness of
equation B lies in two facts. First, together with equation A it
provides a certain symmetry for our system with regard to farm
sector profit maximization.

Second, both these equations are useful in helping to define a
short run Ricardian economy. Chapters 4 and 5 above describe
how Ricardo's production mechanism could conveniently be regarded to function in the short run if we wished to examine
closely the influence of the Corn Laws. But one of the major
characteristics of short run as opposed to long run equilibrium for
Ricardo was that the rate of profits (v) was positive rather than
nearly zero. Both equations A and B help to define the rate of
profits (v). The more intensively each grade of land is cultivated
(as determined by equation A), and the lower the fertility of land
on the external margin (as determined by equation B), the lower
is the profit rate. Just as there is no special reason to believe that
the quality of marginal land is such that profits have fallen to
zero, there is also no reason to believe that each grade of land has
been cultivated so intensively that this long run condition would
hold. Although Ricardo's analysis of the economy's approach to a
stationary state illustrated that the profit rate would fall to zero,

---

*In his discussion of the formation of rent, Ricardo described wheat production
as taking place in this way: "It is only, then, because land is not unlimited in
quantity and uniform in quality, and because in the progress of population land of
an inferior quality . . . is called into cultivation, that rent is ever paid for the use
of it. . . . With every step in the progress of population, which shall oblige a
country to have recourse to land of a worse quality, to enable it to raise its supply
of food, rent on all the more fertile land will rise. Thus suppose land—No. 1, 2,
3,—to yield, with an equal employment of capital and labour, a net produce of
100, 90, and 80 quarters of corn." (*Principles*, in *Works*, 1:70.)

we cannot consider such a position as characteristic of equilibrium in the short run. Because a positive profit rate in the economy is perfectly compatible with equations A and B, they may therefore be satisfied simultaneously in a short run equilibrium model. They show how much land, totally, is used for cultivation and to what extent each quality of land within the total is utilized. They do not assert anything about the rate of profit reaching a zero level.

The extensive margin condition represented by equation B may be represented in a diagram. (See Diagram 3.) The horizontal axis measures the capital/labor input applied to wheat production (x), while the vertical axis measures units of wheat output. Because L as well as x are independent inputs, the production function must be written as:

$$q = f(x, L).$$

The quadrant in which Diagram 3 is drawn is filled with wheat production functions. Each one is drawn with an assumed S-shape, characteristic of eventually diminishing returns. The

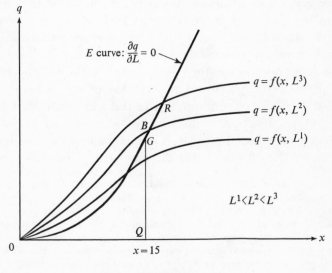

DIAGRAM 3

production curves rise as the amount of land actually cultivated increases. A given amount of capital/labor is assumed to be capable of producing a larger total wheat product when the amount of land placed under cultivation increases.

The E curve is a representation of equation B:

$$\frac{\partial q}{\partial L} = 0.$$

It states that the level of land cultivation is pushed to the extensive margin. A representative point such as G on the E curve is determined as follows:

$$\frac{\partial q}{\partial L} = j(x, L) = 0,$$

which holds at every point on the E curve. This implicit equation may be solved for L in terms of x if:

$$\frac{\partial^2 q}{\partial x^2}, \; \frac{\partial^2 q}{\partial L^2} < 0.*$$

The form of this new equation is:

$$L = b(x).$$

For a given value of x, say $x = 15$, the value of L may be derived from the last equation, such that

$$\frac{\partial q}{\partial L} = 0.$$

This value of L, corresponding to $x = 15$, is denoted $L^{1.8}$. Point G must then be on the wheat production function:

$$q = f(x, L^{1.8}).$$

The slope of the E curve is positive due to the following

*An application of the implicit function theorem.

assumption which seems to be consistent with the description of the agricultural production process:

$$\frac{\partial}{\partial x}\left(\frac{\partial q}{\partial L}\right) > 0.$$

This means that if x increases, the level of land usage, L, such that

$$\frac{\partial q}{\partial L} = 0,$$

must be greater than it had been before x increased. (The extensive margin moves further out if x increases.)

The manner in which the E curve is defined indicates that the only relevant portions of the total production curves drawn in Diagram 3 lie below and to the right of the E curve. This is the region in which:

$$\frac{\partial q}{\partial L} > 0.$$

In the region above and to the left of the E curve:

$$\frac{\partial q}{\partial L} < 0.$$

Production will never take place under conditions of negative marginal product.

SUMMARY

The ideas of an "intensive" and an "extensive" margin in Ricardo's description of production are often mentioned in the literature as part of his analysis of rent formation, but what should also be pointed out is their relationship to his thoughts on

short run profit maximization for a perfectly competitive economy. We have undertaken this task in the current appendix. We
first described how the formation of intensive margin equilibrium
was related to a uniform rate of profit when rent was formed in
the agricultural economy. We then illustrated that profit maximization would be compatible with such an equilibrium if perfect
competition could be shown to hold between the farm firms.
Ricardo made many of the assumptions required for what modern
economists regard as perfect competition in his writings; the only
one he neglected was "no market power." This assumption would
have to be made, however, in order to closely relate the conception of the intensive margin to the optimization condition so
characteristic of the "modern" theory of the firm.

The idea of extensive margin equilibrium could also be related
to the modern theory of the firm if we regarded the quantity of
land as well as the quantity of capital/labor to be an independent
variable. Using this information, we illustrated a condition for
profit maximization which was symmetric to that for the intensive
margin. We further showed that both these conditions implied a
short run rather than a long run equilibrium. Then we illustrated
in a diagram how the extensive margin condition could occur and
what this would mean in terms of standard production functions.
We noticed that taking the extensive margin specifically into account would restrict the region of the production functions on
which output would be defined.

Selected Bibliography

Barkai, H. "Ricardo on Factor Prices and Income Distribution in a Growing Economy." *Economica*, Aug. 1959, pp. 240–50.

──────. "Ricardo's Static Equilibrium." *Economica*, Feb. 1965, pp. 15–32.

Becker, G.S., and W.J. Baumol. "The Classical Monetary Theory: The Outcome of the Discussion." *Economica*, Nov. 1952, pp. 355–75.

Blaug, M. *Ricardian Economics*. New Haven, Yale University Press, 1958.

──────. *Economic Theory in Retrospect*. Homewood, Ill., R. Irwin, Rev. Ed., 1968.

Brems, H. "An Attempt at a Rigorous Restatement of Ricardo's Long Run Equilibrium." *C.J.E.P.S.*, Feb. 1960, pp. 74–86.

──────. "Ricardo's Long Run Equilibrium." *History of Political Economy*, Fall 1970, pp. 225–45.

Cochrane, J. "The First Mathematical Ricardian Model." *History of Political Economy*, Fall 1970, pp. 419–31.

Fay, C.R. *The Corn Laws and Social England*. Cambridge University Press, 1932.

Gootzeit, M.J. "The Corn Laws and Wage Adjustment in a Short-Run Ricardian Model." *History of Political Economy*, Spring 1973, pp. 50–71.

Grampp, W.D. *The Manchester School of Economics*. Stanford University Press, 1960.

Harcourt, G. "Some Cambridge Controversies in the Theory of Capital." *Journal of Economic Literature*, June 1969, pp. 369–405.

Hollander, J. "The Development of the Theory of Money from Adam Smith to David Ricardo." *Q.J.E.*, May 1911, pp. 429–70.

Hutchison, T. "Some Questions about Ricardo." *Economica*, Nov. 1952, pp. 415–32.

Niebyl, K. *Studies in the Classical Theories of Money*. New York, Columbia University Press, 1946.

Paglin, M. *Malthus and Lauderdale—The Anti-Ricardian Tradition*. New York, A. Kelley, 1961.

Pasinetti, L. "A Mathematical Formulation of the Ricardian System." *R.E. Stud.*, Jan. 1960, pp. 78–98.

Ricardo, D. *The Works and Correspondence of David Ricardo*. Edited by P. Sraffa with the collaboration of M. Dobb. 10 volumes. Cambridge University Press, 1951–1955. (Cited as *Works* in this Essay.)

Samuelson, P. "A Modern Treatment of the Ricardian Economy, Parts I and II." *Q.J.E.*, Feb. and May 1959, pp. 1–35, 217–31.

Sayers, R. "Ricardo's Views on Monetary Questions." *Q.J.E.*, Feb. 1953, pp. 30–49. Reprinted: *Papers in English Monetary History*. Oxford, Clarendon Press, 1953; pp. 75–95.

Silberling, N. "Financial and Monetary Experience of Great Britain during the Napoleonic Wars; Part II: Ricardo and the Bullion Report." *Q.J.E.*, May 1924, pp. 397–439.

Stigler, G. "Textual Exegesis as a Scientific Problem." *Economica*, Nov. 1965, pp. 447–51.

Viner, J. *Studies in the Theory of International Trade*. London, Allen and Unwin, 1955.